BE A MOTIVATIONAL LEADER

LEROY EIMS

While this book is designed for the reader's personal enjoyment and profit, it is also intended for group study. A Leader's Guide with Victor Multiuse Transparency Masters is available from your local bookstore or from the publisher.

VICTOR BOOKS®

A DIVISION OF SCRIPTURE PRESS PUBLICATIONS INC.
USA CANADA ENGLAND

OTHER VICTOR BOOKS BY LEROY EIMS

Be the Leader You Were Meant to Be
Keeping Off the Casualty List
What Every Christian Should Know about Growing
Winning Ways

10   Printing/Year   94   93   92   91   90

Unless otherwise noted, Scripture quotations are from the *New American Standard Bible* (NASB), © the Lockman Foundation 1960, 1962, 1963, 1968, 1971, 1972, 1973, 1975, 1977. Other quotations are from the *Holy Bible: New International Version* (NIV), ©1973, 1978, 1984, International Bible Society. Used by permission of Zondervan Bible Publishers; and the *King James Version* (KJV). Used by permission.

Recommended Dewey Decimal Classifications: 301.155
Suggested Subject Headings: LEADERSHIP: EXECUTIVE ABILITY

Library of Congress Catalog Card Number: 80-52904
ISBN: 0-89693-008-4

VICTOR BOOKS
A division of SP Publications, Inc.
        Wheaton, Illinois 60187

**To Lorne Sanny
from whom I have learned
much of what this book contains**

CONTENTS

1 Be a Responsible Leader 9
2 Be a Growing Leader 18
3 Be an Exemplary Leader 30
4 Be an Inspiring Leader 39
5 Be an Efficient Leader 50
6 Be a Caring Leader 60
7 Be a Communicating Leader 70
8 Be a Goal-Oriented Leader 79
9 Be a Decisive Leader 91
10 Be a Competent Leader 101
11 Be a Unifying Leader 111
12 Be a Working Leader 121

PREFACE

A fired-up team is hard to stop. To a band of men and women whose motivation and morale is high, problems appear conquerable, goals seem attainable, and opposition is nothing more than a stepping-stone to success. If, under the power, guidance, and control of the Holy Spirit the leader can develop a warm zeal for the task in the hearts of the people, his job is a joy. But if the people are cranky, cold, and uncommitted, his job is a drag.

What makes a motivational leader? What do some leaders have that inspires people to eager enthusiasim for the work God has given them? Why are some leaders able to arouse in others a high level of morale and commitment? Is it a gift? Or is it an ability that can be learned? I believe it can be acquired and put to work at all levels of leadership. In the home. In the business. In the community. In the church. In tasks large and small. That's what this book is all about.

It sets forth the time-tested keys that the leader needs to unlock the greatest treasure at his disposal—enthusiastic involvement from the people who serve with him. The book is based on the Scriptures, with special emphasis on the teachings of Solomon. I have drawn on my experience as a U.S. Marine in World War II, and from the lessons God has taught me in 30 years of full-time service with The Navigators.

I pray that God will use this book to help develop an ever-growing number of men and women who lead people in joyful and fruitful labor, to the glory of Jesus Christ.

FOREWORD

You're in for a treat!

If you are like me, you don't want an author to waste a lot of time and space getting to his point. Neither do you enjoy wading through pages filled with dreams, ideals, and theories that draw beautiful verbal pictures but lack the ring of reality. Especially when it comes to something as practical as leadership and motivation.

LeRoy Eims writes good stuff. If you haven't discovered that by now, you've obviously not read his other books. His world is the real world and his head is on straight. He faces issues directly, and he isn't afraid to come down on the scriptural side with force and confidence—another rare trait among authors, even Christian authors. But he doesn't bore you with the Bible, either. Where biblical principles fit, they are placed. But they are not forced. I especially appreciate that.

Although LeRoy has been engaged in various roles of leadership since his hitch in the Marine Corps in World War II, including his varied and lengthy involvements on The Navigator staff, I get the distinct impression he is still learning, still listening. He's tough, but he is teachable. Such balance is essential among those who are successful as leaders in today's world. His book will encourage you to develop that same balance in your own life.

You hardly need the reminder that we are living in difficult times. Threatening fears surround us. Instead of meeting the challenge of the 1980s head on, many people are running. Ours is a generation of unmotivated "escape artists." We are desperately in need of relevant, reliable directives from the Scriptures that hold out hope to those who find themselves somewhat paralyzed by the sting of passivity. This book possesses those ingredients.

Like I say, you're in for a treat!

Charles R. Swindoll

I
Be a Responsible Leader

On April 25, 1980, when the 50 Americans had already been held hostage in Iran for 173 days, President Carter appeared on television. In a solemn voice, he disclosed to the American people that a United States military team had failed in its attempt to rescue the 50 Americans held hostage in the American Embassy in Teheran, Iran. After the President described the events which led to the aborted mission, he stated, "It was my decision to attempt the rescue operation. It was my decision to cancel it when problems developed. The responsibility is fully my own."

President Carter realized that where the interests of the United States are concerned, the buck stops at the President's desk.

Responsibility
Whatever the enterprise, the leader is responsible for the success or failure of the mission. But how hard it is for most leaders to accept the responsibility for what happens in their organizations!

In the summer of 1979, the National Aeronautics and Space Administration had a problem. NASA was held responsible for something over which it had little control: Skylab was falling. NASA had built Skylab, bragged about it, and launched it, and now it was in trouble. Tons of metal that had been orbiting the earth would soon come tumbling down. But where? On some-body's head? On somebody's horse? On somebody's house? No one was quite sure. So the world and NASA waited.

To some, the idea of a hunk of metal, nine stories tall and weighing 77.5 tons, crashing to earth was greeted with humor and lighthearted jokes. Chicken Little was paraphrased: "The Skylab is falling! The Skylab is falling!" Parties were given to which guests wore feathers and chicken beaks. Some people wore T-shirts displaying a bull's-eye and the words, "I'm an official Skylab target."

But there was a serious side as well. Many people felt them-selves at the mercy of a force over which nobody had control. Some were fearful. Some were angry. Others grew resentful because the people who were responsible had let the situation get out of hand. They complained that NASA should have thought about this eventuality and made proper plans to bring Skylab back safely.

NASA claimed that although there were some probabilities, they could not predict with any degree of accuracy where the thing would come down. Although NASA was responsible for placing Skylab in orbit, they did not accept responsibility for where it would land.

Motivation and Morale

Let's think for a moment how that event relates to motivation and morale. If a group gets the feeling that their leader is not doing his job—or is not taking full responsibility for what is happening in the enterprise—the members will often become resentful, cynical, or fearful. As they grow dissatisfied with their leadership, motivation and morale will plummet. An incident that occurred in an Amer-ican corporation dramatically illustrates this truth. The administra-tion was in the midst of a personnel problem of tremendous proportions, and the leader adamantly refused to be involved in the solution. By his actions he communicated to his top people that he felt no sense of responsibility for the cause of the problem, nor did he have any interest in leading them through it. The men and women closest to him became frustrated, angry, and despondent. Finally, they confronted the man and told him that because of his failure to lead, they were ready to quit. After a lengthy and heated discussion, the leader was jolted into the world of reality, and promised to do all within his power to resolve the situation. And when the leader accepted his responsibility, the people could unite with him and as a team begin to work together.

Although several factors affect motivation and morale, one of the key factors is responsible leadership. The leader who takes full responsibility for his own actions, and for the people over whom God has placed him, will command their loyalty and respect.

The week after the United States' abortive attempt to rescue the hostages in Iran, I was speaking to a group of servicemen and women at a conference in Virginia. One of the officers told me of a speech given in the Pentagon by a high-ranking general. This general said that the sense of guilt he felt over the failure of the mission was more than offset by the sense of pride he felt toward his Commander-in-Chief for publicly taking full responsibility for the decisions that had been made. The officer who told me the story said that he and the rest of the men and women who served with him at the Pentagon were also greatly moved to rally behind the President. The fact that the President had accepted his responsibility commanded their loyalty and respect.

Rationalization

But all too often the leader is tempted to pass the buck—to squirm out of taking the responsibility for something bad and unpleasant. We all have this tendency. It's part of our nature. For example, if I put on a few inches around my middle, I can easily blame my dad. I can rationalize, "He was a big, heavy man, and I take right after him. If I had had a skinny dad, things would be different. But because my dad was fat, I am doomed to put on weight. It's all his fault." I ignore the fact that I eat ice cream, popcorn, and chocolate-covered peanuts. Somehow that's immaterial. I rationalize that I inherited my proneness to gain weight easily and so can place the blame squarely where it belongs—on my dad.

The Bible has something to say about this kind of phony rationalization. God holds people responsible for their actions. God holds a leader responsible for what takes place in the ranks. The leader is a prime means God uses to keep His people moving in the right direction and doing the right thing. The one who leads the band must face the music.

We can see a clear picture of this principle in the giving of manna to the children of Israel. The Lord had been clear in His instructions. They were to gather on six days of the week, but not on the Sabbath. However, some disobeyed. "And it came about on the seventh day that some of the people went out to gather, but they found none. Then the Lord said to Moses, 'How long do you refuse to keep My commandments and My instructions?'" (Ex. 16:27-28)

Amazing! Had Moses broken the commandments and laws of God? No! Some of the people had, but not Moses. But look whom the Lord held responsible! The leader! God wanted Moses to be ever on the alert, so that sins of the people were not due to neglect or sloth on his part. He wanted the man whom He put in charge to be on top of the situation; for in the final analysis, Moses would be held responsible.

Overcoming Rationalization

Because of our natural tendency to rationalize, we need to recognize this weakness and then battle against it.

Solomon said, "He who is slow to anger is better than the mighty, and he who rules his spirit, than he who captures a city" (Prov. 16:32). It is better to conquer yourself than to conquer others. But conquering yourself is difficult, because you are dealing with your own corrupt, unruly, compromising spirit that so easily justifies its actions and tries to wriggle out of assuming the responsibility for them. Just as allowing yourself the luxury of losing your temper, wallowing in self-pity, or indulging your fleshy appetites is sin, so also, trying to shift the blame for your actions is sin.

When you as the leader fail to deal with sin in your own life, the people who work with you will soon lose confidence in you. If you are the leader, you must arm yourself for a lifetime of fighting against your natural tendencies toward self-indulgence, and your proneness to blame others when you should assume responsibility.

The heart is the field in which these battles are fought. And that is an unnerving thought. "The heart is more deceitful than all else and is desperately sick; who can understand it?" (Jer. 17:9) One mighty truth surfaces in the context of this passage—I am a fool to depend on the strength of my own nature instead of depending on the wisdom and power of God. The heart, being sinister and deceptive, declares evil to be good and good to be evil. We all imagine our hearts to be better than they are. In fact, the human heart will allow us to vindicate ourselves in self-deception. The heart will be the ringleader to camouflage the path to ruin.

But if we turn to God and ask Him to cast light upon our darkness and show us the truth, He will do it. David's prayer is our model. "Search me, O God, and know my heart; try me, and know my anxious thoughts: and see if there be any hurtful way in me, and lead me in the everlasting way" (Ps. 139: 23-24). God knows us. We flatter and justify ourselves, and march blindly toward the brink of disaster; but God in His mercy brings the light of truth to jolt us to our senses.

Accept Responsibility

The application is plain. Whenever I am tempted to succumb to the devious shenanigans of my deceitful heart, I can meet them head-on and triumph over them in the strength of the Lord. If I am responsible for something that goes awry, I must acknowledge my responsibility and set it right. This is not an easy thing to do. The "taking of the city" in physical conflict is child's play compared with the daily, unceasing conflict with my unknowable, deceitful heart. The U.S. Navy has a saying: "It didn't happen on my watch." It means, "I wasn't to blame. It was not my fault." But when God speaks to me and shows me my sin, I had better listen. My heart is always deceitful. God is always true. The choice is mine: I can follow truth or deceit.

If I ignore what God tells me, I am the one responsible, and I will suffer the consequences. "If you are wise, you are wise for yourself, and if you scoff, you alone will bear it" (Prov. 9:12). The aftermath of my actions comes back to roost on my own head. If I behave falsely toward myself or toward the people God has placed in my oversight, I wrong my own soul (Prov. 8:36). I cannot pass the buck to someone else to avoid my responsibility.

When God confronted Adam with his sin, Adam could have said, "Yes, God, You're right." But he didn't. He tried to pass the buck to Eve, but it didn't work. Eve, in turn, tried to blame the serpent, but that didn't work. Trying to weasel out of responsibility is as old as the Garden of Eden.

But chickens do come home to roost. The evil results of poor performance eventually overtake us. The frightening thing is that these results may plague an enterprise for years, decades, even centuries! We are still smarting under the results of Adam's sin.

There are numerous areas where a leader needs to accept responsibility. Solomon addressed five important responsibilities which belong to the leader.

1. Rebuke or correct. The leader must accept responsibility to rebuke sin in the ranks or to correct an improper course of action taken by someone under his charge. At times a leader sees an improper course of action and refuses to correct it because he is afraid he will lose the favor of the people. Solomon said, "He who rebukes a man will afterward find more favor than he who flatters with the tongue" (Prov. 28:23).

2. Act decisively. When the opportunity arises to do something of noble worth and profound consequence, the leader must accept the responsibility to act decisively. Solomon said that if a person excuses unjust behavior by saying he didn't know about it, he will still answer to God who weighs the heart, and renders to every man according to his works. (See Prov. 24:11-12.)

To see a fellow human being in imminent danger, on the brink of disaster, and to do nothing is a crime in the sight of God and man. The people will look upon such a leader as heartless and uncaring or as a coward. However, if a leader spots a need, rolls up his sleeves, steps in, and does whatever he can, his followers will be motivated to join in as well.

When I was in a city in the Southwest of America, I heard a man pouring out his heart for his fellowmen across the sea in Southeast Asia. These people were starving and being brutalized, but their borders were closed to any kind of humanitarian aid and relief. Moved by the need, this man got involved. He called representatives in the United Nations, the Red Cross, various ambassadors of nearby countries, Christian relief agencies, and so on. Everyone said the same thing. "There is nothing we can do. The oppressors are in control. They will allow no one in to bring comfort and aid."

But John did not stop. He began to mobilize a great prayer effort among Christians. I listened to him in a home meeting. The next day his pastor permitted him to lay the burden before the congregation at the Sunday morning worship service. He was on the phone to friends across America and around the world. His plea was that people would pray.

Everyone who heard John was challenged and motivated. And many got behind him and helped him in his effort. He was a leader who commanded love and respect. He saw an opportunity to do something of noble worth and profound consequence and did it. He motivated thousands of people to pray that God might open ways to send relief to needy people.

3. Listen to criticism. The leader should accept responsibility to listen to criticism from the ranks. "He who regards reproof is prudent" (Prov. 15:5), but "he who hates reproof will die" (Prov. 15:10). There is hope for the man who takes his medicine. But if a person is sick, visits the doctor, gets medicine, and then refuses to take it, he might as well have avoided the whole process. Solomon went on to say, "Listen to counsel and accept discipline, that you may be wise the rest of your days" (Prov. 19:20).

Throughout the Bible we see the value of an eager learner's spirit on the part of the leader. But all too often we see the picture of a person closed to counsel and on his way to ruin. If we see this in a leader, we may desert him, and rightly so. God has not given us life to be spent heading in the wrong direction, doing the wrong things, under the leadership of a person who will not listen to wise, constructive criticism.

4. Be honest. The leader should accept responsibility to keep everything open and above board. Recently on the international scene, we have seen giant corporations taken to task for bribery. We see the same problems on the national level, as the sins of leaders are exposed. Solomon spoke to this. "A fool's mouth is his ruin, and his lips are the snare of his soul" (Prov. 18:7). A leader should tell the truth. One of the great kings of France is reported to have said, "If truth be banished from all the rest of the world, it ought to be found in the hearts of princes."

If leaders are not honest, their deception will soon be discovered; and the morale and motivation of the people will plummet.

No one likes to be led by a liar. The man in the ranks hates to be deceived. To be known as a member of a group being led by a liar is humiliating. The lies of the leader reflect on the integrity of every person on the team.

A leader is often tempted to lie to cover up a mistake or failure. However, to do so is madness, for the lie will eventually come to light. His best course of action is to face up to the problem immediately, ask forgiveness of the people, and enlist their aid in setting things right. This is clear evidence that he is taking responsibility for his actions.

5. Be fair. The leader should accept responsibility to deal fairly with his people. "A false balance is an abomination to the Lord; but a just weight is His delight" (Prov. 11:1). Apparently, there was a widespread custom of having different weights and means of measurement for buying and selling—one stone too heavy and another too light. To take advantage of the unsuspecting is an abomination to God and a crime against mankind. Recently, a garage owner told me of a lady who had brought her automobile to him for repairs. For many years she had relied on a certain automobile mechanic to keep her car in good running order. One day this man deliberately did something to the engine to make it run improperly. He then told her she needed major engine repairs. Through a series of circumstances, the lady discovered what he had done. She was angry that he had tried to cheat her out of her money, but more than that she was deeply hurt that the man whom she had trusted for years had attempted to deceive her. The confidence she had placed in him had been violated. She had trusted his judgment and had believed his word. And he had deliberately taken advantage of her trust to use it for his own gain. People rely on a leader in the same way as this woman had relied on the mechanic. And like this woman, when their confidence is betrayed, followers will often turn to another leader.

If any leader is to command a following, he must accept responsibility. That's one of the requirements of leadership. I was greatly challenged one day a few years ago by a sign on the wall of the Manila bus depot. It read, ''The superintendent of the Manila bus depot is responsible for everything that does or does not happen in the Manila bus depot.'' Now that's what I call taking responsibility! How would *you* like to be held accountable for everything that *didn't* happen in the Manila bus depot! But I knew what he meant, and I agreed with him. Had I been able to find him, I would have shaken his hand and complimented him.

Every leader must make a choice. He can accept responsibility, as the Manila bus depot superintendent does, or he can pin the blame somewhere else.

In July of 1979 Moscow was experiencing a spate of shortages on the grocery shelves. That summer there was no Bulgarian jam, no Polish vegetables, no Hungarian chicken. And what did the officials say? They blamed the shortages on the forthcoming Olympic Games!

What kind of leader are you? Are you armed to fight your natural tendency to justify yourself and blame others? Are you trusting God and His Word to help you overcome the deceitfulness of your own heart? Are you listening to what God tells you? God *does* hold His leaders responsible. If you want to lead the band, you have to face the music!

2
Be a Growing Leader

A leader must be sure he is always growing. Continual growth is a key to effective leadership, and God is the key to growth. There are, however, certain things that a leader can do to activate the growth process.

One of the keys to the leader's growth is God's Word (Acts 20:32). But to grow by it, he must spend time in it. As Solomon said, "How much better it is to get wisdom than gold! And to get understanding is to be chosen above silver!" (Prov. 16:16) Notice that it is not just better, but *much* better. This is rather like trying to compare a drinking fountain with Victoria Falls. Or comparing the brilliance of a sunset with the striking of a match. But think for a moment—If you were to ask the average Christian whether he would rather have the opportunity to spend an hour, either filling a basket with silver and gold or reading the Word of God, which do you think he would choose?

I had the misfortune of watching one of the new television game shows on which there was a scheme to carry off as much foodstuffs as possible from a supermarket. The mad scramble practically turned into a riot. The contestants displayed an unbelievable frenzy in their craving for things.

Yet in thousands of homes, the Book that contains the wisdom of God and proper understanding of life goes unopened. Wouldn't it be exciting to see the same hunger for the Word of God as is demonstrated for the treasures of the earth? Both are actually gifts from God, but the gift of God's grace and wisdom should be greatly preferred. Grace involves eternity. The treasures of earth are temporal. Thousands struggle and claw after the wealth of the world and never attain it. (See Prov. 23:4-5.) They spend their lives in frustration.

But the gift of grace and the wisdom of God are never denied. The man or woman who seeks shall find. To the one who knocks, it is opened. The one who asks will receive. Frustration gives way to satisfaction. The soul is at peace. The mind is enlightened, and the spirit motivated by heavenly truth. To trade all of that for Esau's mess of pottage is madness. Yet many do.

Leaders are tempted to give their lives to temporal things, and they need to be alert to the warnings of Jesus. "The one on whom seed was sown among the thorns, this is the man who hears the Word, and the worry of the world, and the deceitfulness of riches choke the Word, and it becomes unfruitful" (Matt. 13:22). The cares of this world can sap the leader's energy. The deceitfulness of riches and lust for glory can divert him. The desire for personal gain and power is there. And all too many succumb to its allurements.

Now and then we see the fall of Christians who were thought to be sturdy oaks in the kingdom of God. What is behind their failure? Many things, but one, for sure. At some point in their lives, they were diverted from those disciplines that encourage personal growth. And when this began to happen, the astute among their followers were devastated, their morale crushed and their motivation brought low.

On a recent plane trip, I was discussing this with a young executive. He told me of the problems his company was facing. Products were being delayed in distribution. There was hostility among the employees, and some had resigned in anger. The business was a mess and the morale of the company was lower than a duck's instep. I asked the young executive what the real cause of the problem was and what he saw as a solution. His words were crisp and to the point. "Our problem is leadership. The man in charge has not grown with the job. When he came to work for us, all was well. He was competent in his job. Now, business has dramatically increased and production is way up. But the top man has remained stagnant. We've got to replace him."

To avoid this type of problem, the leader must continue to grow in both his personal and spiritual life, and in his ability to perform his job. I remember being in a meeting with Dawson Trotman, founder of The Navigators, shortly before his death. He came bouncing into the room with a smile on his face and his eyes dancing. "Let me share a verse with you that God gave to me this morning in my Quiet Time. I don't know how I've lived all these years without this precious verse written on the table of my heart." I was greatly challenged. Here was our leader still setting the example in spiritual growth. Simple things like this motivate people and make for high morale.

Growth is not an option. It is a must. The things I learned in my first year as a Christian are still vital today. I still need to pray, but longer and with greater intensity and understanding. I still need to obey God's direction. Quickly and completely. These are the factors for growth. The basics are basic, and we never graduate from them. Morning prayer and Bible reading are not electives. They are required. Scripture memory and meditation on the Word are still vital to Christian development. And when the people of God see their leader slacking off in these matters, their confidence wanes. Their loyalty lags. Confusion replaces motivation. Lethargy replaces morale, and the enterprise begins to die.

Some years ago I was talking with a leader of a Christian mission. He was complaining to me that the men he had on his team were not following him. Some were not showing up for meetings. They weren't listening to him. Even in their spiritual discussions, the men seemed indifferent to his comments. They had tried to have a Bible study together, but the men began to show up late with their study half done or not show up at all. I zeroed in on this last point—Bible study—because the basics are still basic. I asked him how much time he had suggested as a minimum for study preparation.

"Two hours," he said.

"How much time are you putting in on yours?" I asked.

"Two hours," was his reply.

"You are not growing," I told him. "You were doing that 10 years ago!"

I then challenged him to double the amount of time that he had set as a basic minimum in Bible study preparation. He took the challenge and began to double and at times triple his hours of investment in the Word. The men saw the difference, and their respect and commitment to his leadership took a dramatic turn. When I visited him a year later, I found a band of men committed to the task; their morale was high. The leader's personal spiritual growth was the key to the turnaround.

Enemies of Growth

1. Pride. Solomon wrote, "Pride goes before destruction, and a haughty spirit before stumbling" (Prov. 16:18). The proud man will be brought down. It is not a matter of *if*, but *when*. It will happen either by his own repentance or the judgment of God upon his bloated and haughty spirit. Nebuchadnezzar learned the hard way about pride going before destruction. We are told, "Immediately the word concerning Nebuchadnezzar was fulfilled; and he was driven from mankind, and began eating grass like cattle, and his body was drenched with the dew of heaven, until his hair had grown like eagles' feathers and his nails like birds' claws" (Dan. 4:33). He was a mighty leader of vast armies and hosts of people. Yet pride was his downfall. God will deal with leaders who refuse to give the glory to the One to whom it is due. He well knows how to remind us that "we have this treasure in earthen vessels, that the surpassing greatness of the power may be of God and not from ourselves" (2 Cor. 4:7).

One of the greatest dangers of pride is that it implies overconfidence and in turn breeds a careless attitude toward spiritual realities. When a leader begins to place his confidence in himself, he is on the brink of disaster. His confidence must not rest in the gifts and abilities that God has given him. Yes, he may have a winsome personality, an ability to communicate, and the ability to win the loyalty and affection of others. But where did he get these? The Bible is clear. "For who regards you as superior? And what do you have that you did not receive? But if you did receive it, why do you boast as if you had not received it?" (1 Cor. 4:7)

Recently, I was asked to conduct a weekend conference on discipleship at a lively and flourishing church. I was surprised to learn that just a few years ago the church was practically dead. Scores of the members of the congregation had walked off and joined other evangelical churches in the area. The problem was the pastor. Because he was not a man of prayer, he could not communicate to the congregation the same principles that would help them become men and women of prayer. His shallowness in the Word showed up in shallow sermons and an inability to instruct the congregation in personal Bible study.

Finally, in desperation, the congregation fired the man and began to look for another. Soon they found a man who seemed to have the qualities they were looking for. No, he was not an eloquent preacher or even a very good teacher. He wasn't even a very good counselor. But one thing he had was a deep, sincere, intense love for Jesus Christ which stemmed from his personal devotional life with the Lord. He was a man who prayed many hours and who feasted upon the Word for nourishment for his own soul. Soon after his arrival, a dramatic change began to occur. The congregation began to grow, both in personal depth and in numbers. Some who had quit coming to church returned. People were won to Christ by members of the congregation and brought into the life of the church. Prayer meetings were well attended and real work for God was done as people made prayer a priority.

A dead, demoralized church was brought to life by a humble pastor. The secret? A man of God at the helm, whose total dependence was on God and who led the people into a dynamic fellowship with the Lord Himself. The former pastor relied on himself rather than rooting his ministry in prayer and dependence on God. But a man characterized by humble dependence on God was the catalyst the Holy Spirit used to lead the people to joy, devotion to God, and a desire to win others to Christ.

In your mind, picture a haughty spirit as an army general leading a great army toward the brink of ruin. Who do you see following along after him? Destruction. Bankruptcy. Defeat. Devastation. Annihilation. Catastrophe. Wreckage and the like. Now these are not just words out of Roget's *Thesaurus*. The parade that is led by pride and a haughty spirit *is* comprised of these things. Everytime. Everywhere. Pride and shame are shackled together with a fetter that cannot be broken by anyone but God. And He breaks it when repentance is evident.

Another prominent problem with pride is that it is in direct conflict with the first principle of wisdom, which is to fear the Lord. Also, pride defies the great commandment of God to love Him and our neighbor. This puts the proud man in an untenable position. He is in conflict with himself, at odds with his neighbor, and in defiance of God. "Everyone who is proud in heart is an abomination to the Lord; assuredly, he will not be unpunished" (Prov. 16:5).

If a leader begins to think highly of himself, he and the people with him will soon find themselves in trouble. If he comes to the point where he begins to neglect the Lord and place his confidence in himself, his growth will be stunted and he will begin to shrivel spiritually. And when the people see that, they will lose heart for the work of God.

Remember the words of Christ,

"Abide in Me, and I in you. As the branch cannot bear fruit of itself, unless it abides in the vine, so neither can you, unless you abide in Me. I am the Vine, you are the branches; he who abides in Me, and I in him, he bears much fruit, for apart from Me you can do nothing" (John 15:4-5).

Effective outreach and service are not the result of overwork, but of overflow—the overflow of the life of intimate fellowship with Christ.

Sure, I'll be the first to admit that a leader can be effective if he applies the principles he learns from Dale Carnegie and Madison Avenue sales techniques. But this kind of effectiveness won't last in God's work. The songwriter was accurate when he wrote, "The arm of flesh will fail you." The Prophet Jeremiah wrote,

Thus says the Lord, "Cursed is the man who trusts in mankind and makes flesh his strength, and whose heart turns away from the Lord. For he will be like a bush in the desert and will not see when prosperity comes, but will live in stony wastes in the wilderness, a land of salt without inhabitant. Blessed is the man who trusts in the Lord and whose trust is the Lord. For he will be like a tree planted by the water, that extends its roots by a stream and will not fear when the heat comes; but its leaves will be green, and it will not be anxious in a year of drought nor cease to yield fruit" (Jer. 17:5-8).

When the life of the leader begins to shrivel like a desert bush, the people who follow will begin to do likewise. We reproduce after our kind.

2. *Laziness*. If the leader is too lazy to pray, to study, to seek the Lord, he is once again on the brink of doom. Solomon spoke a clear word on this. "He also who is slack in his work is brother to him who destroys" (Prov. 18:9). The lazy man destroys what he has. He lets what he has sift through his fingers. He casts his God-given gifts and abilities to the wind.

I watched laziness take over in the life of a young man who had great potential for God. I met him when he was a seminary student, showing unusual promise. Most of his professors had high hopes for him. His keen mind, happy spirit, and communicative skills made him the talk of the seminary. Everyone was expecting him to go far. But I wasn't so sure. I was working with him from another angle. I was trying to help him get established in the practice of morning prayer, Bible reading and devotional meditation on the Word—the basics. However, he never quite conquered these areas. He was always too tired to leave his bed and go to his knees. His laziness was his downfall.

Today, 25 years later, he is still in the same condition. A man who had potential for mighty things in the kingdom of God has sputtered along at a haphazard pace. Today he pastors a flock of people who are sterile and powerless. They have not won a soul to Christ in years. The dynamics of discipleship are foreign to their daily lives. They are not motivated to action, and their morale rests on the bottom rung of the ladder. The problem? They have a lazy leader. Solomon's words are to the point. The man who is too lazy to build is equally as destructive as the man who tears down what he has. He is brother to the one who is a great waster. If the leader neglects his responsibilities, he causes as much damage as the man who busies himself in wickedness. Both are destroyers.

In another proverb, Solomon spoke of the danger of sloth and the reward of diligence. "Do not love sleep, lest you become poor; open your eyes, and you will be satisfied with food" (Prov. 20:13). To love sleep is to abuse what God has ordained. Sleep must be used merely to prepare us for further service. Sleep should be the servant, not the master. The lover of sleep will turn into a listless, indolent, halfhearted individual who in no way resembles our Lord Jesus Christ, who did all things well and was consumed with zeal for God. The person who opens his eyes, and overcomes the lazy streak that plagues us all, is promised the satisfaction of the full life that comes from Christ, the Bread of God. Sleep can be a blessing or a curse.

One summer I visited a Navigator Training Program, arriving in time for breakfast. The trainees had been up for about two hours of calisthenics, morning devotions of Bible reading and prayer, and a few early chores. I looked around for the director and was told laughingly, yet somewhat cynically, that he was probably still asleep. I located his cabin and knocked on the door. Sure enough, when he opened the door, he was still in his robe. His eyes were half open, his voice was husky, and he was shocked and bewildered to see me standing there. I spent the day with the program and discovered that morale was plunging, and that motivation was weak. Before the day was out, I had the opportunity to share Proverbs 20:13 with the director. During the rest of the program, he worked to overcome his lazy streak, and because of his diligence won back the respect he had lost.

Allies of Growth

1. Humility. "The fear of the Lord is the instruction for wisdom, and before honor comes humility" (Prov. 15:33). "The reward of humility and the fear of the Lord are riches, honor, and life" (Prov. 22:4).

It is clear from these verses that to walk humbly before God is absolutely necessary to spiritual growth. Such humility reveres the Lord and obeys His Word.

Recently, David Limebear, a close friend of mine from London, England, was touring America on holiday. My wife and I had him as a guest in our home in Colorado Springs. In a conversation one evening, David told of two groups of Christian leaders who had influenced his life. He spent three years around the first group. One person had a serious moral problem. One man was on the verge of deserting his wife and family. One was angry all the time. Another was fed up with life and was contemplating suicide. After David left this group, he joined the fellowship of some people who were quite the opposite. Their lives were a reflection of the character of God, and their homes were characterized by love and joy, patience and kindness.

As David reflected on these two groups, he was able to discern why they were different. The first group sat in judgment on the Bible. They approached its pages to pick it apart. The second group, however, had placed themselves under the authority of Scripture. They obeyed its teachings and claimed its promises.

The contrast was stunning. In pride, the first group set themselves up to judge the Bible. In humility, the second group loved God's Word, and lived under its authority. They were experiencing the riches of the grace of God, and they were being honored by the Lord. They had discovered life.

While David had been around the first group, his morale was zero and his motivation nil. However, David responded enthusiastically to the leadership of the second group, as they set him on the path of productive service for Christ.

Like David, most people respond to a humble leader. They are eager to follow his lead, for they know the hand of God is on him.

They know that his walk with God will strengthen his convictions, strengthen his faith, and deepen his devotion to Christ, and that he will continue to grow.

2. *Godliness.* A person living in sin is obviously not growing in grace and in the knowledge of Christ. Growth comes as he learns the commands of God and by the power of the Holy Spirit applies them to his life. A psalmist said, "I shall give thanks to Thee with uprightness of heart, when I learn Thy righteous judgments. I shall keep Thy statutes; do not forsake me utterly! " (Ps. 119:7-8)

Godliness and growth are so interdependent that one promotes the other. They are virtues that walk hand in hand. Jesus commanded His followers to both learn and follow. To learn of Christ is to grow in His likeness. To follow Him is to live a godly life, to walk as He walked.

"The highway of the upright is to depart from evil; he who watches his way preserves his life" (Prov. 16:17). All who walk the highway of God know that it leads closer and closer to His heart, His will, and His love. That's growth. That's the way to gain strength and stature in the work of God. The Prophet Isaiah had an incisive and interesting comment on this point: "And a highway will be there, a roadway, and it will be called 'the highway of holiness.' The unclean will not travel on it, but it will be for him who walks that way, and fools will not wander on it" (Isa. 35:8).

What a promise! It doesn't matter where we start. We may have little education and few abilities. But if we are diligent in our pursuit of holiness on the highway of God, we will grow in both the wisdom and knowledge of the Lord.

A gifted leader may start out with many advantages over his less endowed brothers and sisters. But if some place along the road he becomes slack in his practice of godliness, his growth will soon be slowed and eventually brought to a halt. The leader must therefore "keep his way" and look diligently to his inner desires and motivations. Growth is unmistakably connected to godliness. By guarding his moral behavior and shunning evil, he is also providing for the blessing of growth in grace and the knowledge of Christ.

If we want to keep growing, godliness must be our lifetime commitment. Note a further comment by Solomon: "A gray head is a crown of glory; it is found in the way of righteousness" (Prov. 16:31). There is no glory in an evil old man. But the man who has walked the pathway of God for many years is encompassed by the glory of God. His wisdom is the result of a combination of study, application, and experience.

When you come right down to it, all the Lord requires of old men and women is that they be disciples. Young or old, the requirements are the same: faithfulness in the basics—in service and stewardship, and in devotion to Him.

Last year, I had the privilege of chatting with Dr. Herbert Lockyer. He was anticipating his 93rd birthday. My wife, Virginia, had baked him an apple pie and we were sitting in his living room enjoying the pie and discussing the things of the Lord. As I looked about the room of this aged saint, the evidences of a life of growth were everywhere. He pointed to the chair where he had his morning prayers. He noted his recent Bible study. His years were a crown of glory, for they had been lived in righteousness.

As I listened to him, I was reminded again that the only way to be found on the way of righteousness is to keep growing. If I don't do that, I will slide into the path of sin and be mired immobile in frustration and guilt.

3. Prudence. "The naive inherit folly, but the prudent are crowned with knowledge" (Prov. 14:18). Here growth and prudence are linked. Prudence is the ability to govern and discipline oneself by the use of reason. Although I must salt my life with periods of recreation and relaxation, the mainstream of my life must be lived among things that make for growth. And doing this is simply the exercise of prudent decisions and judgment. "The mind of the prudent acquires knowledge, and the ear of the wise seeks knowledge" (Prov. 18:15). Note that Solomon added the ear and the heart. What we hear can go in one ear and out the other. But when it lodges in the heart, it affects the life.

Prudence involves our attitude toward knowledge. Solomon had much to say about this attitude. "The mind of the intelligent seeks knowledge, but the mouth of fools feeds on folly" (Prov. 15:14). "He whose ear listens to the life-giving reproof will dwell among the wise. He who neglects discipline despises himself, but he who listens to reproof acquires understanding" (Prov. 15:31-32).

Apollos was an interesting example of this attitude. We are told he was "mighty in the Scriptures." But we are also told that when Priscilla and Aquila heard him, "they took him aside and explained to him the way of God more accurately" (Acts 18:24, 26). Imagine that! A preacher being taught by lay people! It is amazing that they felt the freedom to *do* that. It is also amazing that Apollos had the humility and prudence to listen to them.

The prudent leader will listen to the voice of his followers. In fact, he will create such a permissive atmosphere that the people feel free to talk to him, and are at ease in his presence. If he does this, he opens the door to a wealth of information. This stimulates growth on his part and greater effectiveness in the task, which in turn helps maintain a high degree of morale and motivation.

In the spring of 1980, 162 leaders of The Navigators ministry gathered from around the world, to pray, plan, and ponder the direction of the ministry in the 1980s. Lorne Sanny, the president of The Navigators, led us in our morning sessions. He spoke to the group and then we broke up into discussion groups to talk about what he had said. The leaders of the groups noted the agreements and disagreements and brought them to the attention of Lorne and his leadership team. After a careful analysis of the feedback, Lorne incorporated the comments and suggestions of the discussion groups into his next morning's session. People were delighted to see their suggestions actually being meshed into the framework of the plans for the 1980s. Excitement ran high, and when the conference ended, it was evident that God was sending these leaders back to the four corners of the globe, motivated and committed to the task of helping fulfill Christ's Great Commission.

3
Be an Exemplary Leader

Some months ago I bought a chain saw. I had hopes of using it to cut limbs and logs for the fireplace. When I got it home, I took it to the garage, got it out of the box, and tried to assemble the thing. I read the operating manual carefully. The saw should have been relatively simple to put together; but the more I read, the more apprehensive and confused I became. The assembling guide referred to such things as housing, the guide ban, the lock-off button, the nose, and so on. For the life of me, I couldn't figure out how to put it together.

Today my chain saw remains in the box, disassembled and useless. Now the temperature is down in the 30s, we've had our first snow, and I'd really like to use the fireplace. But because I can't figure out the assembly instructions for my chain saw, everything is at a standstill.

The Marine Corps has a better system than written instructions only. In 1943, I enlisted in the Marine Corps and went to boot camp in San Diego. After the haircut, clothing issue, and a few days of running and calisthenics, I was issued a rifle. I knew nothing about firearms but knew that the Marine Corps would soon teach me to shoot it with some degree of accuracy. I was 18 years old, and thought the whole thing very exciting.

But the morning our drill instructor announced that we were going to learn to fieldstrip the rifle, I was terrified. The thought of taking that rifle apart, and trying to get it back together, seemed too much for my nonmechanical mind. Along with everybody else, I began to undo the screws, and slide this and that in various directions, until I had in front of me a collection of bolts, screws, springs and odd-shaped pieces of metal. The drill instructor was very patient and very clear. Painstakingly, slowly, carefully, he led us through the exercise. He told us the name of each piece, showing us where it fit. He left nothing to the imagination or chance. He led us through the project over and over again. Although most of the guys got the hang of it rather quickly, I didn't. I grew a bit discouraged and began to brood about the possibility that I would never make it as a marine. But the instructor kept at it, and so did I. After a number of methodical, step-by-step demonstrations and explanations, I began to catch on. Soon I could fieldstrip the M1 about as quickly as the rest. We had time competitions, and I began to finish near the top. I was elated. I had mastered the operation.

Then came the shocker. Because there might come a time when we needed to take the rifle apart at night with no light, we were going to do it in time competition, *blindfolded!* Blindfolded!?! Yep, that was right. However, by this time I was up for it. I even had visions of winning. I was excited and eager. My turn came and I went at it with confidence and enthusiasm. Although I didn't win, I turned in a pretty good performance.

What made the difference between defeat with the chain saw and victory with the M1 rifle? Certainly not the *complexity* of the problem. The difference was the personal touch. With the one I merely had a set of instructions. With the other I had a concerned leader who was committed to teaching me something that one day might save my life in combat. I had a person there to help me—to explain and demonstrate the procedure in such a way that even I could grasp it. That's exactly what the people of God need in learning the life of discipleship—someone alongside to demonstrate and to help.

Need for Disciplers

Last spring when I was speaking at a weekend Navigator conference, I had lunch with one of our new staff members. He had
recently graduated from seminary and was looking forward to a
life of fruitful service for the Lord. We were having a discussion
about the needs of new Christians. As we talked, he drew a simple
diagram on a 3″ × 5″ card he had in his shirt pocket. The diagram
illustrated that there are different stages of Christian growth. It
looked like this:

The C represented the point of conversion to Christ. The D represented the point in the Christian's life when he became a mature,
committed, fruitful disciple. He explained to me that one of the
problems he had encountered in seminary was that most of the
students were taught to direct the content of their messages to
people who were mature disciples. They were taught to present the
fine points of Bible doctrine and the intricacies of the faith. But this
type of preaching doesn't meet the needs of new Christians. They
need to be shown *how* to master the basics that help them *become*
the full-fledged New Testament disciples that Jesus talked about—
people who are committed, who love each other, who are continuing in the Word and living fruitful lives. (See Luke 9:23; John
13:34-35; 8:31; 15:8.) Our staff member said he felt that these
young men who were going out to pastor the flock assumed too
much. They assumed that if people were simply *told* to pray, they
would know how to pray; if they were told to study their Bibles,
they would know how to do it; if they were told to witness, they
would begin to witness. He felt that people should be *shown* how to
do these things. I agreed.

To hand someone a Book with over 1,600 pages of fine print and no pictures, and assume he can master it and apply its teachings to his life, is to assume too much. He needs to be shown how. Jesus had to teach His own disciples how to pray. In fact, He gave them a pattern (Luke 11:1-4).

Dawson Trotman realized the importance of this. He would often remind us that telling is not teaching and listening is not learning. He gave us a five-step program to help a new Christian:

- Tell him *what*.
- Tell him *why*.
- Show him *how*.
- Help him *get started*.
- Help him *keep going*.

And Daws would emphasize *show*. "Take him by the hand and lead him through it," he would say.

Need for Patterns

Shortly after I was discharged from the Marine Corps, I was converted to Christ. A few months later, I met Daws. You can imagine how his kind of teaching made so much sense to me. I recalled my drill instructor with his clear instruction and infinite patience and was able to see how that same pattern fit so well into the context of spiritual training.

One of the great needs in the church today is for patterns. All too often the pastor's sermons are directed to people who are disciples of Christ. But what about people who have not come to that point in their Christian growth? What steps can be taken to help them come to the assurance of their salvation? To help them establish the practice of prayer and Bible study? To help them learn how to bear witness for Christ—and eventually train others in these vital matters? Somehow these younger Christians must have their needs met. It seems obvious that what they need is a person who walks through the whole business with them.

If a lady is going to make a dress, what is the first thing she does? She goes down to the store and buys a pattern. Isn't that also the *first* need of a growing Christian? A pattern? The person has just emerged from darkness to light, from the power of Satan unto God. He has repented from sin and turned by faith to Jesus Christ. The Spirit of God has worked a miracle of grace in his life, and he is in a whole new world. "Therefore if any man is in Christ, he is a new creature; the old things passed away; behold, new things have come" (2 Cor. 5:17). Now what? What's the *first* step? Where does he go from here? What does he need?

His need, of course, is for someone to teach him how to walk. "The one who says he abides in Him ought himself to walk in the same manner as He walked" (1 John 2:6). However, that does not come automatically. A person must *learn* to walk with God. But he cannot learn from some *thing*. He must learn from some *one*. When I sat down with my chain saw, I had some *thing*. I had a set of instructions. But when I sat down with my M1 rifle, I had some *one*, a patient, dedicated, concerned leader who was interested in *me*. Oh sure, all of those things you've heard about a marine drill instructor are true. He was tough. He was demanding. But he was also committed to taking a bunch of undisciplined, lazy, half-hearted civilians and make marines out of them. And he did. He was our pattern of a marine.

Why do you think the Apostle Paul told Titus to show himself a pattern of good works? Why did he tell Timothy to be an example of good works? Why was he himself so diligent to set the example and show the way to others? Because that is the *first* need of people.

Need for Continuing Examples

It is not only the new Christian who needs an example to follow. All Christians need the *continuing* example of a godly life lived to the glory of God.

That is exactly what Jesus did for us. "For you have been called for this purpose, since Christ also suffered for you, leaving you an example for you to follow in His steps" (1 Peter 2:21). When a leader sets the kind of example that Christ set, he gains love and respect. Recently at an evening service at our church, I talked with one of our ministers, the Rev. Bill Flanagan. He had just come back from El Paso, Texas where he and a group of young men and women had spent three weeks helping out in a mission church. They had led the Vacation Bible School, taught Sunday School, and spent many long hours fixing up and painting the church. Bill looked a bit haggard, and I asked him if he were feeling OK. He said he had slept on the floor of the church with the rest of the gang for those three weeks, and on the trip back had gone without sleep for 24 hours. He had entered into the hardships with the group and they loved him for it. In spite of all the long hours and relative hardships, they returned to our church enthusiastic, and keenly motivated in the work of God. I'm sure that Bill Flanagan was one of the keys to this.

Bill, who heads up the singles' ministry of our church, some months ago asked me to lead the group in a "Day of Discipleship." We met early Saturday morning and went until late afternoon discussing the life of discipleship. During the lunch break, a few of the men and women gathered around and we talked about the dynamic of their group which is one of the fastest-growing and most enthusiastic segments of our church. During the discussion I asked them why this was so. The answer was on the tips of their tongues—the life and example of Bill Flanagan.

"Oh sure, he is a good teacher," they assured me. "But the real secret is what he *is*, not what he says." Their eyes danced as they related to me various examples of his devotion to Christ and commitment to them as individuals—how he was available to them day or night, how he prayed for them, was patient with them, and accepted them into his life. At one time Bill was the Christian Education director for our whole church, but he resigned this position to direct the singles' ministry and give himself body and soul to them. They know this and love him for it. For Bill, this is a demanding job—long hours and many counseling sessions each week. Bill's cheerful spirit reflects the joy of the Holy Spirit in his life.

Bill's example to the singles of our church demonstrates the truth found in Proverbs 17:22. "A joyful heart is good medicine, but a broken spirit dries up the bones." Think about it. If on the trip to El Paso, Bill had slept on the floor, gone without sleep, and complained about it day and night, what would that have done to the people who were with him? Obviously, their motivation and morale would have plunged. Griping and complaining breeds more of the same, just as a cheerful spirit produces a cheerful spirit and a thankful heart.

Early one cold, wintry morning, I left the house with a bad attitude. The neighbor's dog had kept me awake most of the night. I was hungry and cold. I really didn't want to go to the 6:30 A.M. prayer meeting that was scheduled for Lorne Sanny's team. When I arrived I was grouchy and sullen. In a few moments Lorne walked in. He told us of how the Lord had spoken to him recently from the Word about the importance of a joyful spirit and a thankful heart. He suggested we quote some verses on these topics. He started us off by quoting three or four that had had a profound effect on his life. He not only quoted verses about joy and thanksgiving—he communicated these qualities by the look in his eyes, the smile on his face, and the peace that radiated from his countenance. I was challenged, but remained silent. George Sanchez, Jack Mayhall, and Donald McGilchrist shared a few verses and discussed the implications of the passages.

Soon my heart began to thaw. I was convicted by it all, but mostly by the things that Lorne was communicating by his attitude and demeanor. Solomon wrote, "Iron sharpens iron, so one man sharpens another" (Prov. 27:17). I experienced the sharpening influence of Lorne's example that morning, and God used it to help me in one of the major needs of my life.

If a leader remembers this truth, those who work with him will be affected and their own productivity for the Lord will be enhanced. I have noticed a definite change in my own life as the result of Lorne's example at that early morning prayer meeting—I find that I am more prone to look on the bright side than I was before. This, of course, has helped me in my witness for Christ. It is difficult to speak to another about a life of joy and victory in Christ when you are living in defeat in a crucial area of your own life. All of us need the continued example of a godly life.

Challenge Plus Know-How

There is power in a good example. We can learn things we never dreamed possible when *someone shows us how*. Recently, Professor Sid Buzzell, of the Christian Education Department of the Dallas Theological Seminary, asked me to teach a short course on leadership. During one of the lessons, I asked if there was a girl in the group who had never tied a man's necktie. One young lady raised her hand. I left the podium and walked over to her. I asked her to listen carefully as I explained this very simple process.

"First you hang the tie over your neck with the wide end on the right. Next you pull the wide end down until it is much lower than the narrow end. Then you swing the long wide part up through the gap left between your left wrist and the narrow end and throw it over the top, making sure that you keep a firm grip at the point where the narrow end and the top of the wide end meet. Then put the long wide end down through the 'V' that is formed by the two ends. Then you again throw the long wide end over the top of the point where your thumb and index finger are grasping the top of the two ends and shove it up through the 'V' and then down through the knot, and pull it to its full length and straighten the knot."

After this clear, step-by-step explanation of a simple act, I asked her if she could tie a tie. She just looked confused.

Now let me ask you a question. Which is easier to learn: how to live as Christ's disciple and teach others to do the same? or how to tie a man's necktie? Obviously, it is much simpler to learn to tie a necktie. But even *that* requires a simple demonstration in addition to an explanation. Within 10 minutes I could have *shown* the young lady how to tie a tie. I would have given her one and I would have taken one. We would have stood before a mirror and I would have led her through the process a half dozen times. In fact, that's the way I taught my son, Randy, to tie his tie. But it took more than just telling him how. I went through it with him, step by step.

Challenge without know-how often leads to defeat, and defeat demoralizes. Time and again, new Christians are challenged to witness, pray, study the Bible, and so on. And time and time again, they try and then fail. Why? Because there is no one to show them how. But I have seen thousands of people won to Christ by colleagues of mine who then began to *walk them through* the life of discipleship *step by step*. And the new Christians quickly caught on. They watched, listened, tried it for themselves, and learned.

Just as defeat demoralizes, victory motivates. If the leader will take the time to lead his people through the steps of discipleship, he will have a victorious band of joyful, productive, motivated people whose lives bring glory to God and blessing to those around them.

4
Be an Inspiring Leader

I knew something was different before I even got near the door of the barbershop. As usual the radio was on, but the mellow country and western tunes from our local station were gone. In their place was a brand of music that sounds something like a collison of 1,000 squawking ducks and 100 empty milk cans. When I walked through the door, the noise almost knocked me down. I sat in one of the empty chairs to wait my turn.

The two people who were cutting hair were strangers. Eldon, my barber of 10 years, was nowhere in sight. Instead, there was a young man dressed in jeans and T-shirt, and a young lady in a long, baggy skirt, an embroidered blouse, and sandals. After a while, she called in my direction, "You're next."

When I sat down in the chair, she asked how I wanted my hair cut. I shouted over the noise that I just wanted it shortened up, with very little left on the sides. No sideburns. "Just a good, old-fashioned haircut." She seemed a bit puzzled, but she began. I could tell she had never done anything like that before. Since she was used to long hair, over the ears and down the back of the neck onto the shirt collar, she proceeded to give me that sort of haircut, only modified a bit. I thought possibly she hadn't heard me over the blare of the radio, but I didn't say anything.

39

After she had been snipping away for several minutes, Eldon walked in and came to where I was sitting. It was obvious to him that I wasn't getting my standard haircut. He shouted to the girl that he would show her what I wanted. He raised the chair up to where he could reach my head, turned on the electric clipper and began to cut hair. The girl's eyes grew wider and wider. He took the hair around my ears right down to the skin. Then he chopped a batch off the top, explaining each move to her as he went along. Finally he stopped, turned to the girl, and suggested she finish it up. She smiled and said, "OK." She asked him how to get the chair back to her level, and once I was down where she could reach me, she did the final trimming. With some help from Eldon, she did a pretty good job.

This episode taught me a lesson. No number of years in barber school can prepare a person for every customer. When he leaves barber school, he is prepared to a certain level, but he will need continued development. For some time a barber is going to run into a situation where he needs specific help.

This is true in the Christian life and ministry as well. The leader needs to make sure the people under him are continually growing. The *new Christian* needs the pure milk of the Word, lots of love, protection, the sense of belonging to the family of Christ, training in how to walk and talk, and so on. The *growing disciple* needs the discipline of the daily quiet time, consistent Bible study and Scripture memory, and help in learning how to witness and give his testimony. Also he needs to be introduced to a lifestyle of serving others.

The *budding laborer* needs to be grounded in the great doctrines of the faith, deepened in his life of consecration and holiness, and sharpened in his ministry skills; he also needs a bedrock commitment to the lordship of Christ and clear vision of the worth and potential of each individual. Finally, the *prospective leader* needs special training to prepare him for the rigors of independent leadership when he is on his own. If these groups of people—the new Christians, the growing disciples, the budding laborers, and the prospective leaders—sense that they are under the care of people committed to help them grow and develop, their morale and motivation will be high.

At a gathering of 200 young leaders, I interviewed about half of them. One of the questions I asked was, "Why do you follow the man who heads up the mission in your area?" Three answers were given most often.

• The *vision* that the man was able to impart to them. He had communicated an exciting plan whereby their lives could become significant.

• The *availability* of their leader. When the young people needed counsel or help, the leader was there.

• The *commitment* of the leader. An overwhelming number of these young people said that the reason they followed the leader in their area was because they knew he was committed to help them grow and develop as people—in their spiritual lives. And that was the thing that kept them joyfully engaged in the task. Their motivation stemmed from the deep security that they were not being used, but rather were being helped and nourished, and were becoming better people. The leader was unreservedly committed to them.

He was committed to *their* welfare, not his; committed to *their* growth, not to his greed or self-glory; committed to them, not the task. And because they knew this, they joyfully marched together in the spiritual battle to help fulfill the Great Commission of Jesus Christ.

Qualities of a Leader

To maintain a high degree of motivation and morale, the leader must develop the people involved with him, helping them to reach their fullest potential. And there are several practical things a leader can do to help his people grow. Solomon wrote of four qualities that are vital to a leader.

1. Honesty. The leader must be absolutely honest with his people. "Better is open rebuke than love that is concealed. Faithful are the wounds of a friend, but deceitful are the kisses of an enemy" (Prov. 27:5-6).

Like sheep without a shepherd, people are prone to wander.

They need all the help they can get to stay on the right path. One of the marks of a good shepherd is that he watches over the sheep under his watchcare and does what he can to keep them from the poison weeds, the roaring lion, and the steep precipice.

Rebuke should be given in this same spirit of love and concern. *Open* rebuke means "speaking with free and unhindered honesty." Such honesty may sometimes hurt. However, I'm sure that any of us would rather have harsh treatment from a physician who could help us get well, than gentle treatment from a doctor who could do us no good. A love that is too timid to help a person with his faults is not love at all. A love that wounds us is preferable to a love that neglects to draw us to the Lord. Love must not be silent when the life of a person is at stake. This, of course, is one of the burdens of leadership. But if people know the leader will shoot straight with them and help them when they need it, their morale and motivation will stay up, and their lives can be developed.

One summer I visited one of our summer training programs at the Maranatha Bible Camp near North Platte, Nebraska. As I looked over the program and got to know the teams, I wondered if our program director had made a mistake. One of the team leaders was a matter-of-fact, hard-nosed, plain-spoken individual. On his team were six men who were rather introverted. I was afraid this team leader would drive them further into themselves, and was planning to talk to the program director about it to suggest a switch. However, I just didn't have the freedom from the Lord to do so. I left the program a bit concerned and made this team a matter of definite prayer.

After a few weeks, I returned to the camp to see how things were going. To my happy surprise, I discovered that the team for which I had been concerned was the one the program director felt had the highest morale and esprit de corps. During my stay I talked with the six team members and asked how they liked the program, and how they were getting along with their team leader. They said they appreciated the program and really got along well with their leader. I asked them why they held him in such high esteem. What had he done to win their confidence and respect? To a man, the thing they appreciated was the fact that he did not pussyfoot around with them. He was always straightforward and fair. He commended them enthusiastically, but was not afraid to lay it on the line when they needed correction. To put it simply, he was honest with them. They were a cheerful, motivated team, and very thankful to the Lord for the privilege of being trained by an open, honest leader. "He who rebukes a man will afterward find more favor than he who flatters with the tongue" (Prov. 28:23).

2. *Loyalty*. The leader must stay with the person through thick and thin. He cannot walk off when the person fails in his responsibilities or suffers a setback in his spiritual life. "A friend loves at all times, and a brother is born for adversity" (Prov. 17:17). He cares and stands by the person.

I spent the summer of 1976 in Washington, D.C. One of my responsibilities was to conduct witnessing workshops in various churches in the Washington/Baltimore area. One of these was the Evergreen Baptist Church, a black congregation, located in the heart of downtown D.C. When I arrived at the church on a Monday night, I visited with a deacon who was standing outside on the sidewalk. As we talked, a young lady walked by and the deacon called to her. He reminded her that there was a service at the church that night. She explained that her mother was sick, and she had to care for her. After a rather lengthy conversation with the girl, he seemed satisfied that she was in fact going to take care of her mother and was not just putting up an excuse to miss church. As the girl walked off, he turned to me and said, "They know that if they don't come to church, I will come and get them."

Now that's concern. That's a caring heart of a leader fulfilling his responsibilities. He showed concern for the people in his church even when they weren't concerned about the church. He loved them whether they were doing right or wrong, whether they were living in victory or in sin. Adversity will cement a good leader's love for people, rather than dislodge it. When the disciples forsook Jesus and fled, did He forsake them? Absolutely not. When Jesus knew "that His hour had come that He should depart out of this world to the Father, having loved His own who were in the world, He loved them to the end" (John 13:1).

Jesus' love for us today is just as constant, for He is touched with the feeling of our infirmities. Jesus stays with us in fair weather and foul. When people see a leader manifesting this Christlike trait, their loyalty is firm, their commitment remains solid, and their morale stays high.

This does not mean that their commitment and involvement will never lapse. Even the Apostle Peter failed at one point in his commitment to follow Christ. But through the unswerving love of Christ, Peter came to a place of loyalty and devotion that was so unshakable God could use him to encourage others in their hour of trial. To people who were being falsely accused of being evildoers, he wrote, "Beloved, do not be surprised at the fiery ordeal among you, which comes upon you for your testing, as though some strange thing were happening to you" (1 Peter 4:12). Peter came to the place where he could follow Christ through thick and thin, and maintain a cheerful spirit in it all. Even after merciless beatings, Peter and the other leaders left "the presence of the council, rejoicing that they had been considered worthy to suffer shame for His name" (Acts 5:41). They were unswerving in their devotion to the One who loved them and gave Himself for them. Christ's example led the apostles to respond in kind. Their loyalty was firm, their commitment was solid, and their morale remained high.

3. Generosity. The leader should commend work that is well done. We all need a pat on the back now and then, and a word of encouragement. But praise can have either a good or a bad effect. "The crucible is for silver and the furnace for gold, and a man is tested by the praise accorded him" (Prov. 27:21).

Praise is a great tester of character. If a person is filled with vanity, if he craves self-glory and hungers for recognition, praise will do nothing but fan the flame of his weaknesses. On the other hand, if he is humble and wise, a word of praise can be used by the Lord to stimulate him to even greater service for Christ. Therefore, the leader must know his people and treat each one according to his individual needs.

As a person assumes more leadership responsibility, the leader training that person must teach him to watch out for the dangers of praise and adulation. If the young leader is doing a good job, he can be bombarded mercilessly by the praise of people. Therefore, he must learn to walk a fine line at this point, and accept kind remarks in a spirit of humble grace. But in his soul he must beware of letting others place on him even for a moment the crown that only Christ is worthy to wear. Well-meant but overdone compliments need to be dealt with in the power of the Holy Spirit. No one can do it by himself.

As a leader works to develop the lives of the Christians he is responsible for, he must be governed by basic principles.

• He should be careful in giving praise. Self-love dies hard and the leader can do his brothers and sisters great damage by heaping praise on those who can't handle it. It is no act of love to place weak brothers or sisters under the frown of God.

• He should teach others how to accept praise for what it is—an honest attempt to be encouraging. But he should also recognize the fact that the devil can slip in a drop of poison and do the leader tremendous harm. Praise can be doubly hard to handle if a leader has worked hard and given his best.

• He must teach them that they are only channels. It is Christ in them who gives strength and Christ through them who accomplishes the task.

Just as silver and gold are tested by the furnace, so a person is tested by praise. Saul and David both went through the crucible of praise. "And the women sang . . . 'Saul has slain his thousands, and David his ten thousands' " (1 Sam. 18:7). One failed and one weathered the test. Praise, therefore, is that which the vain leader seeks and the weak leader is hurt by. The true character of the leader is manifested by how he handles praise.

Recently, I was talking with a junior executive in a large corporation. He told me of an incident that took place in his company, and of the effect it had on his motivation and morale. He had been at his desk late one night, and had come in early the next morning. His work load was heavy and he was feeling a bit sorry for himself. Along into midmorning, the phone rang. To his utter amazement, it was the president of the corporation. He had just called to tell the junior executive how much he appreciated all he was doing and to commend him for the excellence of his work. The president's voice was sincere and the man could tell that he really meant what he was saying. The president inquired about my friend's family, how things were going at home, the state of his health, and so on. After a leisurely chat, the president hung up. When my friend told me the story, he looked me in the eye and said, "You know, I really love that man. It means a lot to get an honest pat on the back once in a while."

4. Humility. In all of his effort, the leader must remember that God is doing the training in the lives of the people. "The refining pot is for silver and the furnace for gold, but the Lord tests hearts" (Prov. 17:3).

For a number of years, I was directly involved in our Navigator summer training programs. We would prayerfully plan the programs, select the staff, and choose the trainees. For five to ten weeks we would be together, involved in work projects, Bible studies, preaching sessions, small group discussions, and one-on-one times with the trainees.

In each program we had clear objectives. One program would be geared to evangelism. Another would major on Bible study. Another would have missions as its main emphasis. And so on. Toward the end of the sessions, the leaders would gather the gang together for a time of reflection and testimony to find out what they had learned. It was amazing to see that in many cases, the main benefit they received from the programs was in no way related to the emphases. God had spoken to them in their quiet time or Bible study, and had changed their lives. We learned something from this—we should do our best to develop the people, but always remember that God's training program is running simultaneously with ours.

In every aspect of life, God is the One who works in their lives to train people, and the leader must let the Lord do His work. If he observes one of the flock going through some tough times, there is the tendency to step in and try to carry the person through—to play

God for the person. This is a mistake. The picture in Proverbs 17:3 is of metal in the refiner's furnace. If it does not go in the furnace, the dross will remain ingrained in the metal forever. Outward polishing will not solve the problem. The need is for fire. No mild solution will suffice. The evil that lurks within the hearts of men must be brought to the surface and thrown away. The leader should pray for his people, committing them to the tenderness, love, and wisdom of God. And then he should let God do His work.

Priorities for a Leader

There are two additional principles which are particularly helpful when developing prospective leaders.

1. Choose wisely. The initial key to developing prospective leaders is careful selection of the right persons.

It is a double tragedy to spend time preparing a person for a leadership responsibility only to discover that you have chosen the wrong person. You only have one life to invest and to give it to the wrong people is a waste. Also, to have to go to a person and admit your mistake, and help redirect the course of his life can be devastating. Because he had his heart set on a leadership position, he can easily lose confidence in your leadership, in himself, and in God. It might take months or years to heal the wounds that result from that kind of spiritual injury. So pick the person carefully and prayerfully. Remember, Jesus spent time in prayer before choosing the Twelve (Luke 6:12-13).

As you look for the trainee, keep in mind that some people respond to instruction, reproof, and correction, while others don't. "Do not reprove a scoffer, lest he hate you. Reprove a wise man and he will love you. Give instruction to a wise man, and he will be still wiser; teach a righteous man, and he will increase his learning" (Prov. 9:8-9). Some people are ready for help and counsel, and others are not. But it goes deeper than that—some people have the capacity to be trained as leaders, and others don't.

2. Invest time. The second key, once you have carefully selected the man or woman whom you believe God wants to develop into a leader, is to spend individual time with that person.

"Iron sharpens iron, so one man sharpens another" (Prov. 27:17). This is a vivid picture for anyone raised on a farm. I can still see my dad standing there with his strong-tempered steel file sharpening the hoe, the scythe, the corn knife, and the long-handled shovel. And in this I see an excellent picture of the intense personal contact that is needed to prepare prospective leaders for their job.

Some years ago I had the privilege of being under the tutelage of one of the most productive Christian leaders in the United States. One day we were riding in a car together. I began to criticize a group of Christians and a project in which they were engaged. I had heard someone else talk about their effort, and was parroting what I had heard. Dick sat quietly for awhile, and then turned to me and began to ask me some rather pointed questions. "How much do you actually know about it? Is your information first or secondhand? Do you have all the facts? For instance, are you aware of this? And this?"

I began to squirm and my face turned red from embarrassment. When I tried to weasel out of the situation, he forced me to be honest. After I had made a complete fool of myself, he took a few minutes to tell me the truth of the matter. Then he opened the Scriptures and shared with me what the Bible had to say about my actions. I was chagrined—but wiser, and I learned a valuable lesson. God used that incident, along with a few others that summer, to file down some rough edges in my life.

Possibly you are saying, "But I'm not a sharp individual. Can God use me to sharpen others?" Of course! But first He must sharpen you. One way God sharpens is through other people. Make yourself a student of men and women who are being used by the Lord. You will learn more by studying people than by studying books. Learn to ask questions. Ask these people over to dinner, out to lunch, to play a game of golf or tennis. Spend time with people and study them. Learn by observation. The Spirit of God will use other people to temper and strengthen you and make you a great sharpening instrument in His hands.

God gives the leader the responsibility to develop the people committed to his charge. Without exception, every person under a leader's charge needs further development and training. Each one has been given a gift by God that the Spirit of God can use to enrich and deepen the lives of others for their work of service in building up the body of Christ.

5
Be an Efficient Leader

Last year after our first snowstorm, I decided I needed a new sweater. Since my blue one had holes in both elbows, and my brown one had shrunk, it was time to find a good warm sweater to see me through the winter.

When I arrived downtown, I saw that one of our oldest and best stores was having a giant sale. But more than that—the store was going out of business.

As I was looking through the sweaters, one of the salesmen came over and began to chat with me. I expressed my surprise that the store was closing and asked the reason. He looked at me with a sad smile, and said two words: "Poor management."

I have heard those words so many times. A restaurant closes. . . . A filling station doesn't make it. . . . A land development scheme fails. The reason given is the same. Poor management is one of those behind-the-scenes problems that generally surfaces after it is too late to do anything about it. However, leaders can avoid such problems by knowing and applying the key principles of good management.

Lorne Sanny is the one who first shared these keys with me. I know their value in the international ministry of The Navigators. Let's look at these principles from the context of Scripture.

Receive Direction

The leader's first step is to get a clear signal from God as to what *He* wants him to do. If the leader is doing the will of God, the way He wants it done, and where He wants it done, that leader will be motivated for the task. An awareness that he is involved in the will of God can have an electrifying effect on his soul and spirit.

Recently, I was talking with a man who had been in Christian work for a number of years. His morale had hit bottom and his motivation was nil. He had been in the midst of a big program, working feverishly day and night. Slowly, it began to dawn on him that in spite of all the clanging and banging of the noisy church machinery that spun madly through the week, very little was actually being produced for the kingdom of God. For months he had been swept along at a frantic pace.

When we talked, he began to express his deepest inner feelings. He was filled with doubts and uncertainties. In the eyes of the rest of the Christian community, he was a glowing success, a man to be admired, even envied. But he himself was in a dark and lonely world of doubt. . . . What was it really all about? Was this frantic activity the essence of the Christian ministry? If so, maybe he just didn't fit. He had thought of a number of options. Maybe he should leave the church and follow one of them. He was frustrated and depressed.

Finally, I was able to break into his flood of words. "How much time are you giving to prayer?"

"Not much," he said.

"How much?" I asked.

"Practically no time at all," was his admission.

So we talked about that for a while. By adjusting a few items on his schedule, we were able to find a day when he could drive out by the lake and spend a day alone with the Lord.

We then talked about his Bible study. He admitted it was usually a last-minute endeavor to put some sermons together. Again we raked through his schedule, to arrange some time for personal, devotional Bible study, oriented to application to his own life. He agreed that this was just what he needed, and vowed to make a diligent effort to set aside regular time for prayer and the study of the Word—not primarily for the ministry to others, but to refresh his own soul and spirit.

As the months passed, he stuck with the changed schedule. As a result of his renewed fellowship with God, his motivation and enthusiasm returned. Also, he had a new perspective on his ministry, and developed a deeply settled assurance that he was in the will of God. Naturally, the change affected the church, as its program became less frantic and more productive. Because this pastor was closer to God, he was able to help his people more effectively. His sermons and his public prayers were richer. He was a new man, and his people rose up and called him blessed.

A friend of mine told me about a missionary who was trying to decide whether to go back to the field. He had left the mission station in defeat. The work had been hard, and opposition had made life unbearable. There had been little fruit and much persecution. One of the Christians in his village had been tortured; and as a result of the beatings and inhumane torture, he had emerged from the jail blind and broken in body.

The missionary was in a quandary. . . . Should he return to the field or not? What did God want him to do? To test the leading of God, he wrote on his visa application that he was going to the country to preach the Gospel of Jesus Christ and to win souls for the Lord. He was sure that it would take a miracle for a visa containing that sort of information to be approved.

However, to his utter amazement, it came through. He believed this was of God, and as a result, he gained a new vision for the work, and new excitement about returning. Yes, the climate was still hot and muggy. The housing was still inadequate. Yes, the government was still on a rampage against Christians, and there were still reports of harassment. Trials and afflictions probably awaited him. Yes, he was aware that results might still be meager. But now there was another factor in the equation. He was *convinced* it was what God wanted him to do. And he was filled with keen expectation of what God was going to do.

On returning to the village, he found the people very responsive to the Gospel. While he was away, they had felt a profound sense of shame and disgrace for their part in the persecution. The Christian convert who had been blinded and broken in body had died, and God had used his death to stir within their hearts an unusual readiness to hear the Gospel. At last report, 500 former enemies of Christ were in Sunday School classes studying the Word of God. This missionary had received clear leading from God that he should return. The promise that God made through Solomon had proven trustworthy: "He will make your paths straight" (Prov. 3:6).

Communicate with Your People

Once the leader knows what God wants him to do, he must clearly communicate God's direction to the people and help them see how they fit into the undertaking. This is the second key to effective management. Everyone in the enterprise must know what his job is—what the leader wants him to do.

Moses followed this principle when building the tabernacle. God revealed His will to Moses in clear and explicit terms: "Let them construct a sanctuary for Me, that I may dwell among them" (Ex. 25:8). He went on to say, "Then you shall erect the tabernacle according to its plan which you have been shown in the mountain" (Ex. 26:30). And it wasn't long before Moses gathered the people together and passed along the Word of God to them. "Then Moses assembled all the congregation of the sons of Israel and said to them, 'These are the things that the Lord has commanded you to do' " (Ex. 35:1).

Nehemiah is another example of this process. After God revealed His will to him, Nehemiah was soon in Jerusalem sharing it with the people:

"You see the bad situation we are in, that Jerusalem is desolate and its gates burned by fire. Come, let us rebuild the wall of Jerusalem that we may no longer be a reproach." And I told them how the hand of my God had been favorable to me, and also about the king's words which he had spoken to me. Then they said, "Let us arise and build." So they put their hands to the good work (Neh. 2:17-18).

What happened here? These people had been sitting around looking at a broken-down wall for years. What got them excited about starting this great building project? They had a motivated leader, a man whom God had sent to get the job done. When Nehemiah told them what God had said, and that the king was behind the project, the people became excited.

If the leader wants to maintain his own morale, and that of his people, let him first discern the will of God for himself. Then he must make sure that everyone who works with him knows where he fits in the project, and exactly what is expected of him.

A man said to me, "My boss thinks I'm a mind reader. Recently, he handed me a project and said, 'Work on this.' I did my best and gave it back to him.

" 'That's no good,' he said and gave it back to me to work on again. I tried it from a completely different angle and took it back to him. He was still dissatisfied. So I tried the third time but to no avail. He still didn't like it. The project is still unfinished and I still don't have a clue what it is he wants me to do with the thing."

As I listened to the man, I could tell his enthusiasm and motivation for the project were at rock bottom. I had known him for years and believed he was well able to complete the project if only the boss would tell him exactly what he wanted.

Solomon was a man who did just that. When he needed some timber for the temple project, he went to Hiram and explained what he needed and why. Hiram took the project and finished it in good order.

Later, when Solomon needed some metal work done, he spoke to Hiram about it. Again Hiram's response was positive and the project went off well. The key to it all was clear directions to a qualified man. (See 1 Kings 5 and 7.)

Delegate Responsibility

After Moses led Israel out of Egypt, he was working himself to a frazzle. Jethro, his father-in-law, gave him some sound advice:

Select out of all the people able men who fear God, men of truth, those who hate dishonest gain; and you shall place these over them, as leaders of thousands, of hundreds, of fifties, and of tens. And let them judge the people at all times; and let it be that every major dispute they will bring to you, but every minor dispute they themselves will judge. So it will be easier for you, and they will bear the burden with you (Ex. 18:21-22).

The key phrase here is, "And *let them* judge the people at all times." The leader must first give the followers a job, and then let them do it. All too often a leader will delegate a job, and then meddle and fuss to the point where he has actually taken the task away from the person. This is a classic mistake.

Some years ago, when I was in the middle of a rather large ministry assignment for The Navigators, I sat down with a competent and dedicated man who was working with me, and began to share an idea that would involve him in the project.

After several minutes he stopped me and said, "There is no point in your telling me this."

I was quite taken back and asked why. Was it because he had no interest in it, or was he simply refusing to help?

"No," he said, "it's nothing like that. It is simply that I have watched you, LeRoy, and I know that if I took the project, you wouldn't let me do it. You would poke your nose in, fuss around, begin to change this and that, and pretty soon the rug would be out from under me and you would be doing it yourself."

I argued with him, trying to justify myself. But I came to the point where I had to honestly admit that he was right.

"*Let them* do it." This is a key to motivation and morale. However, there is one qualification to the principle. If the leader wants to release his hands from the reins and let the person get on with the job by himself, he must first select and train the right person for the job. Whether he is choosing people to provide leadership or to do manual work, he should make sure they are able people whom God has qualified for the task.

Solomon had a word of wisdom on this point: "The king's favor is toward a servant who acts wisely, but his anger is toward him who acts shamefully'' (Prov. 14:35). The leader needs to choose a *wise* and *able* helper. ''Like a bad tooth and an unsteady foot is confidence in a faithless man in time of trouble'' (Prov. 25:19). An unfaithful man is a source of pain and discomfort. He will collapse under pressure. So let the leader consider well the consequences of the question, ''Will you let me do it?'' lest he find himself relying on people who are not able to perform.

Be Available

The fourth key is contained in the question, ''Will you help me when I need it?'' To review, the leader must first get his direction from God. Then the people have to know what they are supposed to do. They need the confidence that once they take on a job, the leader will let them do it.

But they also need the quiet confidence that the leader will be available when they need help. This is true regardless of age, ministry, or position in the church of God.

A few years ago, I was at a conference on the West Coast. After I had finished speaking at the Saturday night meeting, I was stopped by a young man who asked if he could talk with me. I explained to him that I already had made an appointment with another man, but he persisted. ''Don't you have just a little time?''

''Well,'' I said, ''we could talk on the way over to the building where I am meeting him.''

''Fair enough,'' he said. He then began to pour out a tale of woe to me that was heartrending. He was in a mess spiritually. He had been a Christian for three years and during those years had become very active in a Christian organization. He had really gotten involved and had experienced good success, and that's when his problems began. He began to give, give, give. Give his time . . . spend long hours . . . pour out his life. But in doing so, his life became shallow and his endurance was stretched to the limit. Finally, he could go on no longer and just gave up. When he heard that I was going to be at the conference, he drove down in the hope that we could talk. He was absolutely burned-out and there was no one to whom he could go for help.

In the few minutes we had, I talked with him about how to become rooted and built up in Christ and established in the faith. As I reflected on the event afterward, I was pained in my spirit. Here was an eager young Christian with a real problem and no one to turn to. And when he heard that there was someone a few hundred miles away who might be able to help, he took the chance that I might have time available and made the trip. Solomon said, "A friend loves at all times, and a brother is born for adversity" (Prov. 17:17). A leader should be a friend who is there in time of need.

Yes, let the people do the work. Don't interfere and don't pester them. But *always* give them the assurance that you are available and eager to help when they need you.

Evaluate Regularly

The fifth key is embodied in the question, "Will you tell me how I'm doing?" It is demoralizing not to know what your leader thinks about your performance.

- "Is it OK?"
- "Is he satisfied?"
- "Does he like what I am doing?"

If these questions are not answered periodically, the person's mind can become consumed with suspicion, imagination, and confusion. When that happens, work is slowed and possibly stopped, because the person is demoralized.

I have seen this so many times in my visits to various areas of ministry, both in the U.S. and abroad. Once I was with a friend who reports to a man in another city. As we talked, he brought up this very subject. "I really don't have a clue if what I am doing is what the boss wants," he said. Then he looked at me and said in a rather plaintive way, "Perhaps you could talk with him, explain what I am doing, and see if he is satisfied."

I had before me a man whose morale was low and whose

enthusiasm for the ministry was lower still. He seemed cut off, and in the dark. His mind was in a turmoil. Was he going to be replaced? He told me about the mental arguments he had had with his boss, as he imagined all sorts of things. I did what I could to get the two men together, to ease my friend's mind, and to help the leader see his responsibilities to evaluate the man's work and honestly tell him how he was doing.

A contrast to this is the way Lorne Sanny handles those of us on the international headquarters team who report to him. We each update our job description and priority objectives every six months. Periodically, Lorne will call me into his office and discuss these with me point by point. "It looks like you're OK here, but these items probably need a little more work," he will say. Then we share something from the Word together, have prayer, and I leave the office knowing exactly where I stand with him. It's a great feeling and it does much to keep me motivated.

When a leader evaluates the work of his people, he *must* have the facts, and know what he is talking about. The leader can profit from the truth in Proverbs 10:31: "The mouth of the righteous flows with wisdom." Nothing demoralizes the people more than to realize their leader really doesn't know what is going on.

Summary

Moses applied these principles of effective management. How did they affect the morale and motivation of the people? One of the best tests of morale among the people is the way they give their time and money to the work of the Lord. If they are disgruntled, disillusioned, and disenchanted, they give little. But if they are fired-up about what God is doing in them, among them, and through them, they give in abundance. In light of that, note Exodus 36:5-7:

They said to Moses, "The people are bringing much more than enough for the construction work which the Lord commanded us to perform."

So Moses issued a command, and a proclamation was circulated throughout the camp, saying, "Let neither man nor woman any longer perform work for the contributions of the sanctuary.'' Thus the people were restrained from bringing any more. For the material they had was sufficient and more than enough for all the work, to perform it.

The work was hard. The hours were long. The living conditions were less than ideal. But the people were motivated and morale ran high.

- Do I have clear direction from God?
- Do I tell my people what they are supposed to do?
- Do I let them do it?
- Do I help them when they need it?
- Do I tell them how they are doing?

Management concerns itself primarily with people—not things. These five questions are vital. They must be answered. More than that, they must be lived out in everyday life. And when they are, the motivation and morale of the people will be secure.

6
Be a Caring Leader

There are various kinds of shepherds and their ideas on sheep tending are not the same. Let's look at two different types of shepherds.

The first one is more of a gatherer than a tender of sheep. He is forever out beating the bushes. He will find a few and then run them into the sheepfold. But his personal *care* for the sheep is minimal. After he gets them into the sheepfold, he loses interest in them. Sensing this, the sheep often wander out the back door and get lost. But this does not seem to bother the shepherd all that much. Daybreak finds him out in the bushes again whacking away; by nightfall he has a few more to add to the fold. However, after a while, some of these also wander off like others before them. As a result, there is very little numerical growth in the flock, and the sheep that *do* stick around are not well nourished. This shepherd's flock is sickly rather than strong and robust.

The second shepherd has a different idea as to how to go about it. Yes, he is equally as eager to add new ones to the flock, but he gives a great deal of attention to them after they are in the fold—diligent, personal attention.

All of us at one time met someone who searched us out and led us into the sheepfold. But our needs did not end there. We needed lots of tender care. We needed to be nourished in the words of faith. Because our problems were unique, we also required individual personal attention. The key to this was not the sheep but the shepherd.

What does a shepherd need to keep the sheep healthy, producing, and reproducing? A number of things are profitable, but two are absolute necessities.

The first essential is a clear understanding of the basic needs of sheep. He must diligently study this, then look over the flock, and determine what his sheep need.

The second essential is his diligence and drive to do whatever is necessary to meet those needs. Solomon articulated it beautifully: "Know well the condition of your flocks, and pay attention to your herds" (Prov. 27:23). In other words, find out what needs to be done and *do it!*

Notice Solomon spoke directly to the shepherd. It is his business to know how the sheep are doing. This is not something he can delegate. The Apostle Paul understood this clearly: "Paul said to Barnabas, 'Let us return and visit the brethren in every city in which we proclaimed the Word of the Lord, and see how they are' " (Acts 15:36). He and Barnabas had completed their missionary journey. Many had come to Christ, as sheep brought into the fold. Now the great apostle proposed a visit to see how things were with them. Were they being fed and cared for? Were the shepherds doing their job? Was there any way he could help? His concern was intense. To the Thessalonians he said, "For now we really live, if you stand firm in the Lord" (1 Thes. 3:8). If they were doing well, his spirit soared with life. But if they were in trouble—sick, hungry, mistreated, succumbing to their proneness to wander—something in him died. His very life was tied to their welfare.

Solomon called upon the shepherd to be diligent. Haphazard sloth is not acceptable. There is too much at stake. Think of the potential of a healthy flock growing and multiplying *forever!* Diligence is the order of the day.

Some months ago, Randy, Virginia, and I were flying from

Belgrade, Yugoslavia to Warsaw, Poland. We arrived at the airport only to discover that the flight was being delayed for about six hours. Randy went immediately to the office of the agent of Yugoslavian Air Lines to get the story and find out what we should do. The agent was full of apologies. It seems there was a group in a town a few hundred miles away who were also going to Warsaw. So the airlines simply sent our plane off to get them. So there we sat. The agent went into action. He arranged a nice meal for us at his expense. He gave us our boarding passes in advance to ensure us seats on an already overbooked flight and had our passports stamped ahead of time so we wouldn't have to stand in the long line at flight time. He also told us to remain in the waiting room until he came and escorted us on to the plane.

When departure time came, he was nowhere to be seen. But we waited. Mobs of people scrambled through the door and hurried to the plane. Finally, he came and walked to the plane with us. When I looked inside the plane, my heart fell. All the seats were taken. But at that moment he unlocked a door leading to the rear of the plane and there was a six-seat first-class section. He ushered us in and spoke to the stewardess, telling her to take good care of us. He was a good shepherd. We were his little flock and he took pains to see we were well cared for. We were on an old, Russian, four-engine propeller plane, filled with loud, happy, pushing, shoving travelers, but we had a quiet, peaceful ride. The agent was diligent to look out for our welfare.

By way of contrast, I was recently on a domestic flight. The steward came by and offered me coffee.

I asked if I could have some hot tea.

"Of course," he said, "I'll be right back with some." Sometime later he came by with coffee refills. He offered me some more coffee.

"No thanks," I said. "I was hoping to have a cup of tea."

"Oh, good grief," he exclaimed. "I completely forgot. I'll be right back." He never came back.

One shepherd was diligent to take care of us, and the other was not.

Enemies of Pastoral Care

What will keep a shepherd from exercising that diligence? It seems to me that four things are enemies of conscientious care from the shepherd.

1. Self-centeredness. Jesus spoke to this trait: The thief comes only to steal, and kill, and destroy; I came that they might have life, and might have it abundantly. I am the Good Shepherd; the Good Shepherd lays down His life for the sheep. He who is a hireling, and not a shepherd, who is not the owner of the sheep, beholds the wolf coming, and leaves the sheep, and flees, and the wolf snatches them, and scatters them. He flees because he is a hireling, and is not concerned about the sheep (John 10:10-13).

Note what the thief and the hireling have in common. They are self-centered, filled with greed and desire for personal gain. Their commitment is toward enhancing their own welfare at the expense of the sheep.

You may wonder why the hireling is involved with the sheep at all. He is there for the money. It's merely a job. When the going gets rough, he runs away.

Are there pastors, missionaries, and Christian workers today who look upon the ministry as a means of personal glory or self-gain? Who regard the ministry as just another profession? Yes, there undoubtedly are. But thank God they are in the minority.

Unfortunately, the thief and hireling will always be with us. And may God help the poor flock that is plagued by such a person.

2. Ignorance. There is a devastating passage in the Old Testament that speaks to this: "For the shepherds have become stupid and have not sought the Lord; therefore they have not prospered, and all their flock is scattered" (Jer. 10:21).

The prophet put his finger on the heart of the problem. If the shepherd is out of fellowship with the Lord, his life will not bless the sheep. There are many reasons for this.

• The shepherd is really only a channel through whom the Lord communicates His blessing to the sheep. Their need for God is greater than their need for the channel. If the leader is not walking with the Lord in the light of His Word, his ministry will be dead.

• If the leader is not studying the Word, he will never learn what the sheep need or how to truly minister to their lives. His ignorance will be a curse to the flock. A wise leader will not only know the general needs of his people, but will also be able to determine their current specific needs.

Recently, I talked with Lorne Sanny about one of his men. I told him I thought there was something that had happened in this man's department that he should be aware of. However, Lorne cautioned me against sharing it at this time. "Wait until his next meetings are over. He has quite a bit on his mind these days."

I was challenged. Lorne is a man with a global responsibility, but he has the time and inclination to keep up-to-date with the men who report to him—even though they are scattered to the four winds. This is *exactly* what Solomon was pleading for. He urged the shepherds to exercise diligence to *know* the state of their flocks. This is no easy task. There is much false and unbalanced religious teaching today through books, magazines, radio, and television. The pastor must keep abreast of what his flock is feeding on. The shepherd has a responsibility to keep the sheep from toxic doses of falsehood and error.

To help the flock grow, the shepherd must know how to communicate the basic ingredients of spiritual growth and discipleship. Many pastors have a problem in this area. They may be great pulpiteers, but the thought of giving individual attention to a person and helping him or her grow is terrifying and mysterious. Why? Because no one ever led them through the basic steps. Much of what they learned in seminary was not geared toward helping individuals. And many pastors have left the ministry for this very reason.

Recently, I had a couple of hours with one of the most motivated pastors I have talked with in years. Six months prior to our chat, he was going to leave his church and go into secular work. He just did not know how to help people grow. Many were coming to Christ and they needed to grow in their faith. His sermons helped a little, but he knew they needed much more than that. He was frustrated, defeated, brokenhearted, and on the way out. But thank God he had a friend who knew how to help people grow. They talked for hours, days, weeks, months. The picture began to clear and he put what he learned to work. Today he has 12 men in his church whom he is discipling. They in turn are nearly to the point where they can begin to repeat the process in the lives of others. Helping people to begin morning prayer and Bible reading, Scripture memory, Bible study, meditating on and applying the Word to their lives, is not difficult.

But two things are musts. First, the leader must be doing these things himself. Paul was clear about this. "The things you have learned and received and heard and seen in me, practice these things; and the God of peace shall be with you" (Phil. 4:9).

Second, he must ask God for a shepherd heart and servant spirit. He will not maintain this sort of ministry for very long without them. He may enter it with a flurry of enthusiasm, but when the realities of spiritual pediatrics are in full bloom, he will be tempted to look for an easier pathway of service.

3. Sloth. Shepherding is hard work. It is a work of faith and a labor of love. A pastor labors in the Word and in doctrine. He labors fervently in prayer. And he must do all he can to ensure that none are lost. He cannot see his flock as a group, but as individuals. Each one needs care, and that is hard work.

What if parents were to look at their children as a group rather than as persons? I have two grandchildren. Four-year-old Joy is strong and active and healthy as can be. The other, Amber Lynn, is a slow gainer. She is a bit underweight and periodically comes down with whatever flu bug or cold virus is going around. What if Becky and Rich were to say, "Oh well, we've got Joy who is robust and healthy; that's good enough," and were to neglect the needs of little Amber Lynn? What if they were to say, "Amber Lynn is too much work; she requires too much attention and time." We would say they were heartless, cold, and not at all Christlike.

That a leader finds his work taxing and time-consuming is to be anticipated. He should acknowledge the fact that leading is highly demanding, and then get on with it.

4. Diversions. I have observed that when a leader commits himself to a ministry of individual personal attention, a host of other opportunities wait in the wings to lure him off the track. Glorious opportunities! He must examine these opportunities under the light of his main job and calculate his priorities very carefully. The ministry of discipling people and meeting their needs can look rather dim in the bright light of things that are big, noisy, and accompanied by a flare of excitement. There is little glamour in the day-to-day work of caring for the welfare of people.

In a meeting of mission directors in San Diego, the phrase, Glorious Opportunity became a catchword. It all began one morning, when one of the men spoke of the glorious opportunity he had had that past week to serve the Lord. He described the event in glowing terms, going on and on about his involvement in the glorious opportunity. Finally, the man who was chairing the meeting asked a pointed question.

"It all sounds quite fascinating and exciting, but what does it have to do with the mission that God has given our organization?"

A silence fell on the room as they looked at the first man, awaiting his answer. He seemed a little confused and finally he blurted out, "Well, probably nothing—but it *was* a glorious opportunity!"

During the rest of the week, the men chuckled from time to time about the incident. But they also thought a great deal about the implications of the question and answer.

I have been impressed that whenever Lorne Sanny gets his top leadership together, the first thing he does is to review with us the objectives of our mission. In fact, Lorne says that his primary responsibility is to help set, clarify, and maintain the objectives of our organization. I agree. And the reason, of course, is that it is so easy to be diverted into some Glorious Opportunity that appears.

There are three ways you could destroy your life. One is to do nothing with it, to give in to that lazy streak in you and just sit idle while the world and its terrible needs go weeping by. The second is to give yourself to the wrong thing; to fight and claw after something for an entire lifetime, only to discover, finally, that you have given your life to the wrong thing. The third way is through diversions. You are generally on the right track, but you periodically observe some Glorious Opportunity that leads down a bypath, and follow blindly after it.

Opportunities to Meet Needs

There is great need for Christian leaders who will take the time to learn the needs of their people and then meet those needs. Self-centeredness, ignorance, sloth, and diversion all fight against the leader who would set his heart to feed his flock. But by God's grace, anyone can become a diligent leader who looks out for his people.

During World War II, I was stationed for a time at Camp Pendleton near San Clemente, California. We used to go to Los Angeles and Hollywood when we had weekend passes. In Hollywood in those days there were men known as zoot-suiters. They wore suits with extremely long coats and baggy pants that were pegged at the ankles, gaudy wide-brimmed hats, and gold watch chains that practically dragged on the ground. One weekend a gang of them got together to have some fun beating up on marines. Fifteen or twenty of them would find a lone marine and pound him senseless. It was great fun for them, and they clobbered a half dozen marines on that weekend. The commander of our base was horrified. So the next weekend any marine who wanted to volunteer for extra duty was told to fall out in dungarees and boots. They were loaded in the back of a truck and driven to Hollywood. All weekend they drove the streets of Hollywood looking for zoot-suiters. When they found some, they hopped off the truck and dealt with them. From that weekend until the end of the war, there was no record of a marine being attacked by zoot-suiters in Hollywood. While the commander's method was questionable, it was obvious he was looking out for the welfare of his men.

One time when I was in the Denver Airport on my way to Wichita, Kansas, I noticed an unusual number of airline personnel gathered at the gate where our plane was to load. A large group of boat people was about to arrive from Los Angeles.

I watched as scores of confused and hesitant people came off the plane. They were wearing badges, carrying plastic bags given by the Red Cross, and wondering where to go and what to do. However, they didn't have to wonder for long, for relief workers and airline personnel were there to meet them. Many of the relief agency people and the airline personnel probably had never heard of Solomon's advice about paying attention to the needs of the people committed to their care. But they were doing it. Some refugees were wearing badges marked "Lutheran Immigration and Refugee Service." Others were wearing large black and yellow pins with the letters U.S.C.C. Some were carrying plastic bags reading "Donated by German Red Cross Federal Republic." One worker was especially efficient. She would note their badges, lead them to the proper gates, ask them to sit down, and then swing into action getting their boarding passes, pointing out the restrooms, and making sure they were properly informed as to when the next flights would be. All in all, the workers were terrific. Soon the refugees were smiling, relaxed, and at ease. They knew they would be cared for.

When people know someone is taking care of them, they will normally respond as these refugees did. A leader who looks out for the welfare of his people will have a group of followers who are motivated and eager to follow him.

A friend of mine recently visited our home in Colorado Springs, shortly after he resigned his commission in the air force. Since Ray had been teaching at an air force leadership school for the past two years, we spent a lot of time talking about leadership and its effect on morale and motivation. During one of our conversations, he told me about his first squadron commander, Lt. Col. Billy J. Brown. He noted that Colonel Brown's most notable quality was that he took care of the people in his squadron. Because of the nature of their jobs some of the aircrews were required to spend long periods away from home. While these crews were gone, often for three months at a time, Colonel Brown was diligent to check with each of their families weekly to see if they had any needs.

Another aspect of the squadron's mission required each aircrew to be away from home for seven days every three weeks throughout the year. During this time, the crews were restricted to a certain area of the base, and separated from their families. Frequently an aircrew member scheduled for restricted duty faced a potential problem at home—his wife expecting a child during his restricted duty, or a sick child who needed to be hospitalized. In such cases, Colonel Brown always kept in touch with these men and their families and monitored the situations closely. In addition, he always scheduled a backup crew member to cover for these men if an emergency did arise. All of the crew members knew that most of the commanders on other bases refused to meet individual needs like this. Ray told me that because of this personal concern, the men in his squadron felt that Colonel Brown was deeply interested in their lives, on and off the job. Their problems were his problems. As a result, morale was high and the men were motivated to do their best for him. They didn't mind working long, hard hours or even pulling extra duty, because they knew Colonel Brown would take care of them.

By way of contrast, Ray told me about other commanders who produced the opposite effect. They didn't meet the personal needs of their people, and as a result, morale suffered. Based on his discussions with hundreds of officers during his tour as a leadership instructor, Ray concluded that the first concern of young officers in the air force today is whether their superiors are really looking out for the welfare of their people or simply taking care of themselves. He observed that on bases where commanders were going out of their way to take care of their people, morale and motivation were high. However, on bases where commanders were not doing this, resignations were high instead.

A leader must watch out for his people and tend to their needs. Solomon said, "Know well the condition of your flocks and pay attention to your herds." God has called us to be shepherds. Our Master's words to Peter should be enough motivation for us: "Do you love Me? . . . Shepherd My sheep" (John 21:16).

7

Be a Communicating Leader

During the summer that Virginia, Randy, and I spent about a month behind the Iron Curtain, the only news we heard was from Radio Moscow. A man with a lovely British accent would give the news broadcast from Moscow. As he told of the inhumane and treacherous deeds of the U.S. Air Force in Africa, he said, "The drone of their bombers drown out the denials of their president." Week after week we were fed the Communist party line. It was depressing and disturbing.

Finally, the day came to fly from Prague, Czechoslovakia to Geneva, Switzerland. We arrived at the hotel, went out for a bite of lunch, and then headed for the newsstand. We located *Newsweek*, *Time*, and the *Herald Tribune* and then returned to our room and read each of them. Because we were starved for the news of what was happening in the world, we made a daily trip to the newsstand. Like most people, we had a craving to be informed.

A Leader Informs

Whether we're talking about international events or the workings of a group of people, we all like to be informed. The leader must be conscious of this need of the people with whom he is working.

Dawson Trotman was a master at keeping people informed.

During my early years with The Navigators, all of us at the International Headquarters were instructed to keep Thursday nights open. On that evening each week, we would gather in the living room of Daws and Lila's home at Glen Eyrie, and Daws would brief us. He would read letters from the missionaries and have reports from the reps who happened to be at the Glen. He would also just share with us current blessings from the Word— what God was teaching him. Then he would bring us up-to-date on his current thinking, plans, ideas, and forthcoming projects. He especially enjoyed announcing engagements. He would drag out the announcement to keep us in suspense, and finally reveal the happy news.

I look back on those evenings with fond memories, for they were the highlight of the week. God used those times to keep our morale high and infuse us with a great sense of excitement and gladness. Even though my job was not all that important in those days, Daws made me feel that I was necessary—to him, to the ministry, to accomplishing the task, to the Great Commission. Yes, it took time, effort, and thought on his part to weld us into a team. We were the "Nav family," his and Lila's "Dear Gang." And we felt it.

Keeping people informed is Godlike. God could have left us in the dark about how the world came into being, but He didn't. "In the beginning God created the heavens and the earth" (Gen. 1:1).

He could have left us in ignorance about how sin entered the world, but He didn't. "Then the Lord God took the man and put him into the Garden of Eden to cultivate it and keep it. And the Lord God commanded the man, saying, 'From any tree of the Garden you may eat freely; but from the tree of the knowledge of good and evil you shall not eat, for in the day you eat it you shall surely die' " (Gen. 2:15-17).

He could have left us to speculate about the origin of the Bible. But He didn't. "All Scripture is inspired by God" (2 Tim. 3:16a). "For no prophecy was ever made by an act of human will, but men moved by the Holy Spirit spoke from God" (2 Peter 1:21).

We were not left to our imaginations about these things, for we might have dreamed up all sorts of theories. But God in His mercy turned on the light. He chose to reveal to us the great mysteries of the universe. Why do you suppose He did that? Because *it is His nature* to keep His people informed. For some reason He wants us to *know*. It is His way of doing things. "He made known His ways to Moses, His acts to the sons of Israel" (Ps. 103:7). The leader will do well to remember this. Any group, any organization, any board of elders or deacons, any corps of Sunday School teachers functions better if it feels it is up-to-date and "in the know."

I once read of a professional athletic team that was losing games. Morale and motivation were low, and there was bickering and strife among the athletes. When a reporter probed into the situation, he discovered the root cause: the players did not know what the management was thinking and so they fed on rumors. Was the club going to remain in the city where they were playing or would they be moved across the country? Were the players secure in their jobs, or would they be traded? Was the owner going to fire the manager? And on and on. Nobody had answers. Just questions. Team members felt suspicious and anxious, and this affected their game. They knew they weren't playing well, and this made them mad because they knew they could do better. And their poor performance angered the coaches. And so on around the circle. Their real problem was a management problem. Their leaders were not doing their jobs.

It is interesting to note that the Apostle Paul used teams of people to dispense information. "As to all my affairs, Tychicus, our beloved brother and faithful servant and fellow-bondslave in the Lord, will bring you information. For I have sent him to you for this very purpose, that you may know about our circumstances and that he may encourage your hearts; and with him Onesimus, our faithful and beloved brother, who is one of your number. They will inform you about the whole situation here" (Col. 4:7-9). It was important to Paul that people knew what was going on, who was going or staying where, and how different ones were getting along. Note how frequently things like this appeared in his letters: "Erastus remained at Corinth; but Trephimus I left sick at Miletus"

(2 Tim. 4:20). "Timothy my fellow-worker greets you; and so do Lucius and Jason and Sosipater, my kinsmen" (Rom. 16:21). "Only Luke is with me" (2 Tim. 4:11).

What was he trying to accomplish by all of this? To help all of these people feel part of the movement? To muster prayer support? To keep them motivated? To make them feel important to the work of Christ? Probably all of these things and more. And any good leader today will do likewise.

My first independent assignment with The Navigators was to work in a student ministry in Pittsburgh. After my wife and I had moved there, we heard that The Navigators were attempting to purchase Glen Eyrie in Colorado. Humanly speaking, this was an impossibility, for we had six weeks to raise $100,000, which amounted to almost half of our annual budget. It was more money than we had ever dreamed of raising. But Daws believed that he had the mind of God in the matter, and mobilized the staff to action. I was new to the staff, hardly knew anyone, and didn't really feel a part of the team as yet. But Daws soon changed all that. I began to get letters from him telling me how the campaign was going. I wrote frequently, sending in the money we were able to raise. He was thankful and enthusiastic, and his spirit was catching. Soon I found myself swept along in the momentum. I knew I was having a part in a modern-day miracle.

A Fool Withholds Information

Solomon says, "The lips of the wise spread knowledge, but the hearts of fools are not so" (Prov. 15:7). The *Authorized Version* uses the word *disperse*, which means "to scatter or diffuse." A wise man spreads the word, while a fool does not. I have been involved in various undertakings where secrecy seemed to be the order of the day, and for the wrong reasons. In one instance, information was withheld because it made those who had it feel superior to those who didn't. It was a status symbol, and those of us who were on the outside looking in felt inferior to the group who knew things we didn't. They were the "in-group;" everybody else was a second-class citizen. This is devastating to morale and demoralizing to those who are treated in such a shabby manner. As a general rule, it is better to disperse knowledge than withhold it. That which is communicated with humility and prudence is a blessing to all who receive it. *People crave information that bears on their lives*—and the wise leader knows how to communicate it with wisdom.

A few years ago, I personally experienced the effects of withholding information from people. My wife and I were in Fiji for a ministry assignment at the University of the South Pacific in the city of Suva. We flew back to Nandi to take a plane to New Zealand where I was due to speak at a men's retreat the coming weekend. But there was a problem. The airplane workers who fueled the planes at the Auckland, New Zealand airport were on strike. Nothing was flying from Fiji to Auckland. Day after day we walked to the Nandi airport to ask about the situation, but they were unable to tell us a thing. Then one day we got a phone call. There was a Pan Am plane coming through with some seats available on a first-come, first-served basis. The next morning we were at the airport. We weren't first in line, but we were close. We checked in and were issued boarding passes. But more problems. No one was quite sure how many seats were empty. For days we had been held in suspense. No information. Now, with boarding passes in hand, we were *still* in suspense. Would we get on? No one knew. So we waited. We prayed. And believe it or not, even after the plane was in, no one could tell us yes or no—go or no go. It wasn't until we walked in the door of the 747 that we were *certain* we would be leaving. It was a strange situation—full of suspense and anxiety. The one thing we needed was information.

A Leader Continuously Informs

In the summer of 1976, when I had the privilege of speaking at the morning worship service of the Evergreen Baptist Church, I was amazed to see a 14-year-old boy reading the Scriptures, giving the announcements, and leading in prayer. The pastor was sitting beside me and I asked him about it. He explained it was a practice he had followed for many years. That week it was the turn of the youth department to lead the service. Next week the ladies of the church would lead, the following week the men, and so on. His statement was significant: "When I leave here, they will know as much about running a church as I do." Here was a man who was dispersing knowledge among his people.

It is especially important for a leader to *brief the people at the beginning of any project*. This will help him find out how *they* feel about it. If they are enthusiastic to begin, they can then appoint a few from their group to work with the leader in formulating plans. After some time when the leader senses he has the backing of the people and the mind of God on the matter, he should call the group together and lay out the plan.

• Here's what we're doing and why.

• Here's how I feel God would have us go about it, and what we need to do to accomplish the task.

• Here are my suggestions as to people who should take responsibility for various phases of the project, and reasons why they are suggested.

• Here's what it's going to cost us in time and money.

• Here's when I hope to have the work completed.

The leader should spread the word to all who will be affected by his decisions. And he should do everything in his power to keep the people with him at each phase of the endeavor.

The leader must keep in mind that people crave information, and are pleased when they are kept up-to-date. "Pleasant words are a honeycomb, sweet to the soul and healing to the bones" (Prov. 16:24). How many things do you know of that are both healthful and sweet? Not many. We are told from our childhood, "Don't eat that, it will make you fat. . . . Don't eat this, it will rot your teeth. . . . Don't eat that, it's not good for you."

But not so with pleasant words, for they are both sweet *and* healthful. When the leader applies this principle, he will discover that the people will enjoy getting the information and they will be a healthy lot—motivated, with their morale at a high peak.

Solomon offered advice about the kinds of information that are valuable.

1. Timely information. "A man has joy in an apt answer, and how delightful is a timely word!" (Prov. 15:23) The timely word is a blessing—both to the giver and receiver, and the leader will find joy in sharing that which is helpful. But there is a *time* to speak. Quite often the leader's words are not as effective as they might be because they are ill-timed. There is "a time to be silent, and a time to speak" (Ecc. 3:7b). If a leader jumps the gun and shares before the people are ready, he errs. If a person waits too long, the rumor mill may take over. And when rumors are flying rather than truth being dispersed, the enterprise can be in big trouble.

James reminds us that much damage can be done by the tongue. "The tongue is a small part of the body, and yet it boasts of great things. Behold, how great a forest is set aflame by such a small fire! And the tongue is a fire, the very world of iniquity; the tongue is set among our members as that which defiles the entire body, and sets on fire the course of our life, and is set on fire by hell" (James 3:5-6). While much damage can be done by the tongue, when it is used right, it disperses a blessing.

2. Accurate information. The leader is preserved by both mercy and *truth.* "Loyalty and truth preserve the king, and he upholds his throne by righteousness" (Prov. 20:28). When a leader practices telling his people the truth in every situation, stability and confidence develop. But if people are never sure if they are being told the truth, the whole operation becomes shaky. People will not knowingly follow a liar. Deception and falsehood are death to the leader.

Recently, a friend told me of an incident that illustrates this point. This pastor of a church was frequently called upon to go to other churches to conduct evangelistic services. When he would return to his congregation, he would report the results. But there was a problem—his reports were always exaggerated. What his parishioners heard from people in the churches where the pastor had visited always differed from the pastor's reports. Some of the members of the congregation he pastored found it funny, but others found it unnerving. "If he lies to us about this," they said, "possibly he is lying to us about other things as well." They began to resent it and soon they became convinced they should get rid of him. A vote was taken and he was fired. Followers must be able to depend on the leader's word.

3. *Appropriate information*. A leader can sometimes share too much information with people. There are certain things that are better kept quiet or shared only with a few. If the leader shares certain things with new Christians, it can do them spiritual damage. They may have no way to relate to the information, and could become offended. It could plant seeds of doubt or fear in their minds; if they take it wrong, they could become angry or bitter. Here again we see the importance of the leader knowing the people with whom he is working. Solomon said, "The tongue of the wise makes knowledge acceptable" (Prov. 15:2). *That's* the essence of the point. A leader should share what the people can accept, assimilate, and understand.

In 1958 I was running a Navigator ministry in Lincoln, Nebraska. A number of young leaders whom my wife and I were training were living in our home with us. One of them came to me and asked if one of his friends could move into the home for a couple of weeks. It was spring break at the university and he had no place to stay. I was against the idea. He was a brand new believer and the environment of our home was pitched at a high level of Christian maturity. But Bob pressed the point. He thought it would probably do his friend a lot of good. Rather than make a big thing out of it, I finally agreed, against my better judgement.

The guy moved in, and it wasn't long before he began to resent some of the things that we were doing. Early morning prayer . . . early morning Bible study . . . conversation that was way over his head. He became sullen. In a few days he moved out. He just wasn't able to assimilate the things we did and discussed. Rather than being built up by his stay, he left very discouraged. While the leader should normally be open and share freely with people, there are some times when he must cautiously select the information he disperses to certain people.

4. *Motivating information*. Solomon had keen insight here. "The heart of the wise teaches his mouth, and adds persuasiveness

to his lips'' (Prov. 16:23). This is one of the most powerful verses in the entire Bible on the subject of motivation. When a leader's words are motivated by his heart, they are persuasive. When the leader merely quotes General So-and-so, or Doctor Somebody, the words do not have the same punch as when he says, ''Here is a truth that I have experienced in my life,'' and then goes on to share his heart.

All of us can tell the great difference between a person who merely speaks what he has read or heard and one who shares what he has felt and tasted. The timely truth that is dispersed must come from the heart. There must be conviction undergirding the knowledge that is shared. The heart is the best communicator. When the heart is teaching the lips of the leader, it adds persuasiveness to his speech. There is conviction, life, warmth, sincerity—what is commonly termed *heart*.

Communication takes thought, effort, and planning. But it is well worth it.

8
Be a Goal-Oriented Leader

Never in her entire life had the lady shared her faith in Jesus Christ with anyone. She was approaching middle age and had a burning desire to witness. But the whole thing seemed a bit out of reach. She was living a fine Christian life, but she simply did not know how to start, what to say, or how to go about it.

Our group had been invited to conduct a witnessing seminar at her church. When this lady learned of the seminar, she was ecstatic. She had prayed for years that she would be able to get some practical help in becoming an effective witness for Christ. Maybe this would be the answer to her prayers.

On the night when the seminar began a rather large crowd assembled. There was an excitement in the air. We had been holding these seminars every week all summer in the Washington D.C. area, and this was the largest group of the summer.

So we began. The plan was simple. I gave a brief description of the two-night curriculum and then shared a few passages from the Scriptures on the importance of witnessing. I told them our overall goal was to teach them how to tell others how to establish a relationship with Jesus Christ and that we would teach them step by step how to do this. Our first night was spent teaching the people how to give their testimonies. Since most had never done this, we went slowly, simply, and methodically through the Scriptures about the subject. Our key passage was Acts 26, which records Paul's personal testimony before King Agrippa.

We broke the class into small groups and our team went to work. One member of the team helped each person formulate the salient facts regarding his or her conversion experience and Christian growth. The lady had a rather ordinary yet powerful story. After she thought it through, a team member helped her write it out. She really caught the drift of what we were doing and entered into the spirit of it with great enthusiasm.

Then we dropped the bombshell. Their homework assignment was to go to a friend, a neighbor, or a relative and tell him the story. Although some were a bit nervous, the assignment didn't seem to shake this lady at all. She had waited for years for help like this, and she was eager to get her toes in the water.

We reassembled the groups, sang a hymn, had prayer, and dismissed. It was around 9:00 P.M. As the lady left, she thought to herself, *Why should I wait until tomorrow? My boss is working late. Why not go to the office and see if he will listen to my story?*

So she caught a downtown bus, went up the elevator to the office, and, sure enough, there he was. He looked up, surprised to see her.

She told him that she was taking a seminar at the National Presbyterian Church, and that part of her assignment was to give her testimony to someone before the second session the next evening. She asked if he would like to hear her story.

"Sure," he said. "I'll get some coffee and take a break and listen." So she began. She told him what her life had been like before she had accepted Christ. Then she told him of the circumstances surrounding her conversion and what the Lord had done in her life since that time.

As she finished her story, the man turned pale. Visibly shaken, he said, "What I have heard tonight must be why I was spared." And he told her this story.

Some years before he had been invited to a cocktail party, and on the way he had had not one, but *three* flat tires and had missed the party completely. Most of the people at the party had died of food poisoning. He knew God had spared his life. Now here was this friend telling him this marvelous story of her salvation in Christ.

"That's wonderful," he said. "But how can I experience this for myself?"

"Oh," she said, "we haven't learned that part yet. That comes tomorrow night when we learn to share the bridge illustration. You'll have to wait until then."

The next night we began our second seminar by asking the students to share with the rest of the group what had happened when they gave their testimonies. The lady stood and told us the story. I had never seen a person so motivated to learn how to explain the Redemption Story. She took careful notes, got it all clearly in mind, and when the seminar ended, headed back downtown to tell her boss the rest of the story. She was well on her way to becoming an effective witness for Christ. She had been shown a goal that was attainable. It was a simple thing—well within her reach. We helped her attain the goal; and as a result, she happily moved ahead in witnessing.

There is an important principle embedded in this little story. People need goals and they also need help reaching them. Often the situation calls for them to set their own goals and a timetable to reach them. On occasion—as in a classroom situation—they have the goals and timetable set for them. But in either case, people need goals at a level where they can reach them. Good leadership does what it can to help people set these goals, monitor their progress, and keep moving ahead on time, on track, and on target.

Setting Goals
Goal-setting is a foreign idea to vast numbers of people. So the leader often must move very slowly as he introduces the concept to the people with whom he is involved. Why do people need goals? Three reasons come immediately to mind.

1. Direction. People need goals to provide direction for their lives. It is impossible for a person to press toward the mark if there is no mark. It is impossible for him to finish his course if there is no finish line.

Let's say the State of Colorado is sponsoring a mountain-climbing contest. Thirty competitors show up in Boulder to take part in the big event. They gather together and the sponsor of the event arrives, to give them instructions. All he has in his hand is a starting gun. "Okay," he says. "Go!"

"Go? Where? Which peak? Longs Peak? Pikes Peak?"

The room is filled with loud complaints. No one knows where to go or what to do. Even though they may be the top 30 mountain climbers in the nation, they are immobilized if they don't know which mountain to climb. They can't function. The people of God need goals to provide direction.

2. *Progress*. Goals are important to insure progress. Without them, the people can be like rocking chairs, with movement but no progress. An absence of goals can endanger the life of the church. The church machinery may function in a whirl of activities—committee meetings, ladies' circles, and the like—but if there is no primary goal toward which the body of believers is striving, the program may be feverish but going nowhere.

3. *Accomplishment*. The third reason for goals is to accomplish a purpose. He who shoots at nothing hits it. If I have no goal, I will never know when I am finished. I can work day and night for weeks, months, years; but without a specific goal I will never complete the task. Why? Because there is no task. I have not set out to do anything measurable. Therefore, I never get anything measurable done.

Even though these are good reasons to set goals, some people feel the whole notion of establishing goals is unspiritual. Somehow it sounds like work done in the energy of the flesh. "And we all know where *that* leads and how much *that* sort of thing can accomplish for the glory of God!"

Goals and Scripture
However, as we look into the Scriptures, we do find evidence of well-thought-out plans and objectives. In 1953 I moved to Pitts-

burgh to launch a campus ministry. It was my first assignment and I needed direction. One of the passages the Lord gave me was 1 Corinthians 2:1-5:

And when I came to you, brethren, I did not come with superiority of speech or of wisdom, proclaiming to you the testimony of God. For I determined to know nothing among you except Jesus Christ, and Him crucified. And I was with you in weakness and in fear and in much trembling. And my message and my preaching were not in persuasive words of wisdom, but in demonstration of the Spirit and of power, that your faith should not rest on the wisdom of men, but on the power of God.

In the margin of my Bible I wrote, "Claimed for ministry in Pittsburgh, June 25, 1953."

As we look at that passage, we note that Paul had a predetermined plan that he had carefully thought through. He also had a practical goal in mind. His plan: to preach Christ crucified. His goal: that the faith of the Corinthian Christians should rest on the power of God.

One of Nehemiah's objectives in building the wall was that they might "no longer be a reproach" (Neh. 2:17). Solomon said in his prayer of dedication of the temple,

"Hear Thou in heaven Thy dwelling place, and do according to all for which the foreigner calls to Thee, in order that all the peoples of the earth may know Thy name, to fear Thee, as do Thy people Israel, and that they may know that this house which I have built is called by Thy name" (1 Kings 8:43).

Christians should most assuredly ask the Lord for specific guidance about specific plans that move toward specific goals. Paul pressed toward the mark. He said, "This one thing I do." He had a goal.

Long-Range Goals

The leader should help his people first focus on their long-range objective. For unless they have evaluated their overall life goals, they have no basis for determining more immediate, everyday goals. That, of course, is the problem in the lives of most Christians. Like their unsaved neighbors, they may have certain long-range goals for which they are striving in the everyday affairs of life. They may have set goals in the area of financial security, physical health, a happy family life, and so on. But it never occurs to most believers that they must set certain long-range goals for themselves spiritually, if they are to accomplish anything for the Lord, or become the people God wants them to be.

Goals can vary; but unless the person has long-range goals burning in his heart, he will have no basis for setting his spiritual activities on a daily basis. His long-range goals determine his short-range goals.

Short-Range Goals

Once a person has determined his long-range goals, the leader should help him determine the short-range goals which will help him meet his objectives.

A track star had to learn to take his first step, like any other child. When he was learning to walk, the parents held out their hands and encouraged their child to venture forth on that awesome first step. And then the magic moment came when he let go of everything and took that first unaided step. The parents stayed close with smiles, assurances, and urgings. They were only a step away. It would have been foolish for them to have tried to make the child walk the length of the room. That came later. For soon he was walking by himself, and then running, jumping, and skipping. And finally, under the supervision of a track coach, he prepared for the Olympic games.

Short-range goals are essential in accomplishing long-range goals. For instance, let's say the leader has a new Christian in the fellowship whose primary goal is to become a man of God. What will the leader do? Encourage a great leap forward? No, he will suggest things on a short-range basis that are in direct line with the new Christian's long-range goal. For instance, the leader might suggest the practice of morning prayer and Bible reading. Why? Because he knows that those things are in direct line with the objective. So are Bible study, church membership, Scripture memorization, and meditation on the Word. One of the leader's jobs is to help the person select realistic goals for himself; and usually this means toning down overambitious goals that would prove too difficult to reach.

When I was working as a representative of The Navigators in the Midwest, I often made trips to Oklahoma State University. One of the new converts I met was Carl McCutchan. Carl was a new babe in Christ and eager to grow. Joe Lee Holt, the man who had won Carl to Christ, had suggested that Carl read the New Testament. So Carl began. He became so engrossed in the New Testament that he began to neglect his university studies. He read through the New Testament again and again—eight to ten times a week. He couldn't put it down. His grades began to drop and he almost flunked out of school. When we found out what was happening, we had to go to Carl and help him strike a balance. We didn't want to cool his ardor for Christ, but neither did we want him to flunk out of school. So we helped him set some attainable goals that helped him remain in college and grow spiritually as well.

Last winter our family went to Steamboat Springs for a few days of skiing. Randy took his camera along to get some pictures of some of the activities on the slopes. We got shots of him doing various daredevil jumps—exciting maneuvers called the Back Scratcher, Tip Drop, Mule Kick, and Helicopter.

As I looked at the pictures, I was reminded of his first few times on the slopes when Mark Sulcer took him and a few of his buddies and taught them the basics: how to snowplow on the bunny slopes, how to turn, how to parallel, and so on. Very easy, very slow and simple stuff. But those things were necessary to his becoming the sort of skier who could speed down any slope on the mountain. These were easily attainable short-range goals that were in direct line with his long-range goal—to become an expert skier.

Short-range goals are necessary for motivation and morale. Solomon said, "Desire realized is sweet to the soul" (Prov. 13:19). Breaking a project down into small, bite-sized units that are reachable keeps a person going. Frankly, that is why I usually suggest that a person begin his study of the New Testament by studying a few of the shorter books. At a chapter a week, it only takes three weeks to complete the Book of Titus, four weeks for Colossians, five weeks for 1 John, and so on. Once a person has actually completed a study of a few of the New Testament books, he can then launch out on one of the longer ones. But if a person starts with Matthew, it is 28 weeks before he has studied even one book. However, if after only three weeks there is that "desire accomplished" of having actually studied a whole book of the Bible, the person will most likely be motivated by accomplishing his goal. After some years the person will have studied the entire New Testament; but to begin, he or she needs that incentive of a desire accomplished. "Hope deferred makes the heart sick, but desire fulfilled is a tree of life" (Prov. 13:12). Delay can mean discouragement. It is important to help a person attain some goals, to give him the sense of accomplishment and help him gain momentum.

People need help in determining God's goals for them, and then in making God's goals their goals. Solomon said that desire accomplished is sweet to the soul. However, not *all* desire accomplished is sweet to the soul. Note Psalm 106:15: "So He gave them their request, but sent a wasting disease among them." A parallel passage to this is Ecclesiastes 2:10-11:

And all that my eyes desired I did not refuse them. I did not withhold my heart from any pleasure, for my heart was pleased because of all my labor and this was my reward for all my labor. Thus I considered all the activities which my hands had done and the labor which I had exerted, and, behold all was vanity and striving after wind and there was no profit under the sun.

From these passages we can see that satisfaction comes in achieving those things that God lays on our heart. Fleshly desire accomplished is void of satisfaction. It is hollow, filled with disappointment. But, the fulfillment of something that God has impressed on our spirits is indeed sweet to the soul.

Goals and Fulfillments

Solomon suggested how to insure that goals will result in a sense of fulfillment and satisfaction. He said, ''Commit your works to the Lord, and your plans will be established'' (Prov. 16:3).

The leader must teach his followers to actively seek the will of God and to base their plans on God's will. Solomon no doubt learned this from his father David, who said, ''Commit your way to the Lord, trust also in Him; and He will do it'' (Ps. 37:5).

There are two reasons for committing plans and programs to the Lord. First, all of our plans are to be for the glory of God. He must give the plan and receive the glory when it is accomplished. Second, our plans are too heavy for us to bear alone. In fact, the word *commit* literally means ''roll them upon Him, as a burden too heavy to be borne by yourself.''

To proceed with God-given plans in faith, humility, and total dependence on Him, with an eye to His glory alone, is the sure path to success. God has given us the responsibility of planning. ''The plans of the heart belong to man'' (Prov. 16:1). The word *plans* suggests the idea of placing things in proper order. We see the same word picture in the story of Abraham who ''built the altar there, and arranged the wood'' (Gen. 22:9). God gave man his brain and He expects him to use it. Planning and organizing— placing things in proper order—are responsibilities placed squarely on the shoulders of those who serve God. Good leaders will teach their followers how to do these things.

Goals and Persistence

Teaching a person to determine God's goals for himself, and to stick to those goals, is not always an easy task for a leader. It is all too easy for a follower to be swayed by others and to let them influence his goals. The Apostle Paul warned, ''Let each one examine his own work, and then he will have reason for boasting in regard to himself alone, and not in regard to another'' (Gal. 6:4). Paul pictured a man who looked back at this life and felt good about what he saw. He had not been motivated by unhealthy comparison with another person.

It is difficult, however, to keep from letting others influence our thinking, and to listen to God alone.

Not too long ago, a friend of mine talked with a group of seminary students about the basics of the Christian life. As they talked, these men expressed that their biggest sense of defeat during their years in seminary stemmed from their failure to consistently maintain a program of morning prayer and Bible reading and personal Bible study. As my friend talked with them further, he found that as they were caught up in the academic system at their school, they began to compete for better grades in their courses. When they looked around at other students and saw them getting better grades, they began to spend more time studying to improve their grades. Soon they found their lives so absorbed in academics that they no longer had time to meet God personally everyday. While these men knew a personal relationship with God should be the number-one priority in their lives, they had altered their goals and made their number-one priority achieving good grades. Comparing themselves with their peers sidetracked them from one of God's goals for them.

Paul's words apply: "So then each one of us shall give account of himself to God" (Rom. 14:12). Since we are accountable to God, our goals should come from Him.

The leader must help his people keep this perspective. He can help the person set reasonable and attainable goals. However, he must not try to cram his ideas and standards down their throats. He needs to let *God* speak to them, and let *God* show them what is right at their present level of growth and commitment. Then when they achieve the goals they set, they can rejoice and thank the Lord. If they do not achieve them, they can go to the Lord and ask for His continued forgiveness and strength. They are responsible to God in the matter.

Goals and Action

The leader's responsibility doesn't end after he has helped his followers set long-range and short-range goals. Next he must show them how to put those goals into action.

1. Timing. It is important to teach them when to act. It is equally as dangerous to dart ahead too quickly as it is to lag behind. *When* to do something is of equal weight and consequence as *what* to do. Just a few weeks ago, I was discussing this very thing with the president of an international Christian mission. He had gotten a letter from a director in the field that told of a plan they were contemplating. They had their goals carefully set and were seeking his advice. They were eager to get underway and asked that the president read their letter and then give them a telephone call, hopefully to give them the green light to move ahead. As we discussed the matter, the president said, "I think they are on the right track but their timing is off. They are about a year ahead of themselves. My advice to them is going to be to wait."

The importance of proper timing cannot be overstated. Even though people feel a strong urge to plunge ahead, they must be taught to temper their emotions with wisdom and discretion.

2. Implementation. The leader must make sure the people know how to implement the goals they have set for themselves. To know *what* to do and *when* to do it, but not to know *how* to do it breeds frustration. I was discipling a young potential laborer a few years ago and we were confronted by this problem. He had struggled for months about resigning from the air force. I sat with him night after night in his barracks as we discussed the pros and cons. The decision seemed to shift back and forth. One night it would look like the obvious thing to do was stay in the air force. The next night, it would seem better to resign. Back and forth it went.

Finally, after months of prayer and discussion, he determined it was the will of God for him to separate from the air force. His goal was to serve the Lord as a missionary overseas. He planned to leave the service and pursue that goal. But then we faced the next problem. What should his timetable be for all of this? When should he leave the air force? So again we prayed and discussed it night after night, sitting on his bunk in the barracks. After some months the fog lifted and he saw the answer clearly. He would get out the following summer and go to college in the fall. But where? There was a school in Nebraska he could attend. And there was one in his home state of Illinois. But the more we talked about it, the more he seemed to feel he should attend a college on the West Coast. I made a few telephone calls to a friend of mine who lived in Los Angeles and my friend was able to help him work out the details of housing and employment. It seemed that the goal was set, the timing was decided, and all was well. But then the whole process hit a snag. His girlfriend in Illinois was against the idea, and he began to waver. So I encouraged him to commit that matter to God in prayer; the Lord worked out the situation beautifully.

And I learned that it was not enough to help him set his goals and establish a timetable—I also was responsible to help him diligently pursue the goals he had set.

9
Be a Decisive Leader

In the fall of 1951 our family moved to Seattle, where The Navigators were providing counselor training and follow-up for a Billy Graham Crusade. I was assigned to work in the counseling room, which meant that I set up chairs and placed counseling materials beside them, made sure the chairs were dusted clean each night, ran errands, and so on. Those were exciting days—I was a fairly new Christian and it was a thrill to see the people stream forward each night when Dr. Graham gave the invitation.

Each night after the meeting was over, part of the small Navigator team took the decision cards and went to work. They sent each person a letter of encouragement. Pastors, whose congregations were near the homes of these people, were notified. The team worked long into the night, night after night. After several days the guys and gals began to get a bit weary. One night after a particularly large response, the gang was working into the early hours of the morning. They had been at it for many hours, when one of the night watchmen stopped by. He was a friendly type. "How's the crusade going?" he asked. One young Navigator looked up through bloodshot eyes and answered hoarsely, "Oh, the meetings are going great. But these decisions are killing me."

What he meant, of course, was that it was a lot of work to get those letters out that same night to all of those who had responded to the invitation to receive Christ into their lives. But those of us who heard the story applied it in another way as well. The phrase became a catchword among the staff. Whenever we were faced with a particularly difficult decision as to which plan to follow or what route to take in the area ministry, we would be reminded of the truth of that phrase. It was not the ministry itself that was difficult. In fact, we all loved the opportunity to be involved in the work of evangelism and of helping new converts grow. But when difficult decisions came along, we responded the way the follow-up worker responded to the question of the night watchman. "The ministry is going great. But these decisions are killing me."

Decisions Are Difficult

Many leaders feel the same way. They love the ministry, but the decisions they must make are often the most difficult aspect of their work. Recently, I received a letter from a man responsible for a large missionary program. Since the country where he is serving is not likely to renew his visa, he must decide whom to recommend to take his place as the leader of the ministry.

Not long ago I talked with a chaplain in the armed forces. He had received an invitation from a church to be its pastor. Should he stay in the military or leave?

A pilot in the air force has been on the phone with me a number of times telling me of his dilemma. Because of his outstanding soul-winning ministry among his fellow officers, many feel he should leave the air force and go to seminary. They feel he would be an outstanding Christian leader and could profit immensely from seminary training.

Why is decision-making such a difficult thing? Last week I sat down with my family and asked them if they ever had difficulty making decisions. They said, "Yes." So I asked them what made this so difficult. Here's a list of things they mentioned:

1. *Confusion about the will of God.* Often it takes many weeks, months, or years to discover God's will for your lives on a particular issue.

2. The desire to hurt no one. Some decisions carry with them consequences that affect the lives of many people. You may dislike the idea of bringing discomfort to anyone else.

3. A distaste for unpopularity. This can affect everything, from what clothes you wear to whether or not to witness. Some decisions bring unfavorable reactions.

When they finished, I decided to add a few things to that list.

4. Too busy—no time to think the matter through.

5. Cowardice—simply afraid to step out and decide.

6. Ignorance—don't have all the facts you need to make the decision.

7. Pride—if you are consumed with pride, you will not be a straight thinker. Your mind will not reveal the *best* plan but the plan that will bring the most glory to you. Making the right decision is often difficult, but the right decision is an imperative. One wrong turn on a drive from Minneapolis to Dallas could result in your missing the entire state of Texas! Texas is hard to miss but you could do it! You could end up in New Orleans or Los Angeles. So it is in decision-making. A wrong decision can send you down a blind alley or on a road that leads to destruction. Decision-making is an art that you as a leader must master. There is nothing that lowers the morale of people more than to follow a person who consistently leads them down wrong paths.

How Do You Make Good Decisions?

How can you insure that you will make good decisions? Some of the basic elements in decision-making emerge from the Scriptures. Solomon said, "There is a way which seems right to a man, but its end is the way of death" (Prov. 16:25).

1. Recognize bad decisions. It's important to realize that, as a human being you are prone to making bad decisions. Jesus spoke of this: "They will make you outcasts from the synagogue; but an hour is coming for everyone who kills you to think that he is offering service to God" (John 16:2). Paul admitted to the same problem. "I thought to myself that I had to do many things hostile to the name of Jesus of Nazareth" (Acts 26:9).

It is easy to settle for what "seems" right and walk in self-delusion. For that reason Solomon warned, "He who trusts in his own heart is a fool" (Prov. 28:26). The Prophet Jeremiah described the human heart as the great deceiver (Jer. 17:9). Who among us would repeatedly place our trust in one who constantly lies and deceives? Yet that is what many do. The leader must not permit himself to fall into this trap. Since we have within us the potential for every sin, every wrong decision, every foolish act, every bad judgment, every false step taken since the dawn of history, it behooves the leader to look outside himself when decisions present themselves.

It was a bad decision that led Eve to follow the advice of the devil. It was a bad decision that led Aaron to make a golden calf. It was a bad decision that led David, the man after God's own heart, to wallow in the slime of immorality, murder, and deceit. It was a bad decision that led Solomon to worship false gods and become involved with strange women. The nature of mankind is to make bad decisions. This can apply to the simplest of things.

In the spring of 1977 I was asked to be the speaker at a Navigator weekend collegiate conference in Indiana. When I arrived, I was met by a couple of staff members who told me that many more collegians had come than they had anticipated. For that reason, all the bedrooms were full. They had reserved a bunk for me in a room with three of the staff. Without thinking or asking questions, I said, "That will be fine."

What I didn't realize was that the room was barely big enough for one person. Also, I did not know that we were located right beside the hallway door—which squeaked and banged. And I didn't realize that the other three guys in the room snored very loudly. In fact, among the Indiana Navigators, they were known as the Chain Saw Gang.

I had arrived a bit tired, so Saturday night I retired early. About 11:30 or 12:00 they came in and went to bed. Each of them began to snore. A variety of sounds—rolling thunder, wet dribble, whistles, deep throaty noises—woke me up and kept me awake. After trying to sleep through it all, I finally took my blanket and went out into the dining room where there was a plastic davenport up against the wall. I lay down on it around 4:00 A.M. and had just gotten to sleep when the cooks came in at 5:00. I made a bad decision. As I look back on it, I realize I could have saved myself a lot of trouble by asking a few questions, assessing the situation, and making a more sensible decision.

2. *Define the problem.* To make good decisions, you must ask yourself, "What's the real issue here? What's the real problem we're trying to solve?" My need at the conference was sleep. I assumed that if they provided a room, I could get some sleep. But that wasn't the case. A simple question such as, "Will it be quiet enough to get some sleep?" would have shed the light I needed to make a good decision. There was a small, inexpensive motel just down the road that would have been available and given me what I needed. My decision seemed right. But it wasn't.

The words of Paul ring clear: "Therefore be careful how you walk, not as unwise men, but as wise" (Eph. 5:15). Paul suggested that we are to look at all sides. That's the admonition that the leader must heed—look at all sides of the problem—study the issues and assess the situation, before the decision is made. To adequately assess the issues, the leader must try to get all the facts, an abundance of accurate information.

3. *Listen before answering.* Even if you think you already know what to do, it is wise to probe for more light. "He who gives an answer before he hears, it is folly and shame to him" (Prov. 18:13). The best way for a leader to deal with an issue is to first *listen* to all the facts.

I was recently in a meeting of the International Leadership Team of The Navigators. As we met day by day, we discussed a wide variety of important issues that affect the ministry. One day we spent many hours discussing the many facets of a particularly knotty problem. At the end of the day, Lorne Sanny thanked us for a good day of hard work. He then said, "When I came into the meeting this morning, I had what I thought to be a solution to the problem. But thanks to you men, I now have a great deal of added light and I can see the issues in clearer perspective. I'm sure we are now on a better course.'' He did not answer until he took the time to listen.

Often the leader fails at this point. He doesn't want to listen to something with which he disagrees. Pride enters in and he believes he knows what is best.

Job's friends failed at this point. Job, on the other hand, took the time to investigate the case which he did not know (Job 29:16). Potiphar failed to get the facts when his wife lied to him regarding Joseph (Gen. 39:17-20). The folly of answering a matter before the facts are known was forbidden by the law of God (Deut. 13:12-14).

4. Offer suggestions to brainstorm. After you have satisfied yourself that you know the real issues, you are ready to take the next step in decision-making. Now that you have isolated the real problem, you should gather your advisors and let them offer whatever they feel to be the best solution to the problem.

Solomon stated it precisely. ''Without consultation, plans are frustrated, but with many counselors they succeed'' (Prov. 15:22). A leader must provide a permissive atmosphere so that people feel they have the liberty to offer whatever they think might work. A leader should let them brainstorm.

If a leader is fortunate enough to have people around who will offer suggestions, he is blessed indeed. A wise man realizes he is limited in his understanding. He knows he needs help. Many minds applied to a problem will in all likelihood see more facets than if just one person wrestles with it. And as they talk it over, more ideas will come. It is interesting to note that the word *consultation* means generally the same as the Hebrew word *sod*, which refers to the tackle of a ship used in its steering and handling. Counsel provides direction for a leader. Any enterprise needs a great deal of guidance and advice to insure proper direction. The whole picture here is that of a leader giving deference and paying close attention to the godly counsel of his advisors. During consultation, the group should look for various paths, for a number of solutions. They should focus on alternatives.

There are many advantages to this exercise, even in the simple matters of everyday life. Let's say the old automobile has finally come to the point where it needs to be replaced. And let's say there is a teenage son in the family who has recently gotten his driver's license. The dad wants a medium-sized, four-door—pure vanilla. The son thinks a hot sports car would be the thing to get. What will the dad do? Tell his son to be quiet? Tell him his idea is stupid? No. If he's smart, he will spend a few weekends with his son visiting the car dealers, talking it over, looking at all the angles—family trips, vacations, grocery shopping, insurance costs, the whole lot. In all likelihood they will both adjust a bit and come to a decision that suits the entire family.

There are several advantages to bringing in others to talk over a decision. First, there will be greater *cooperation* in carrying out the decision if the people know they had a hand in the decision process. Another is *enlightenment*. Obviously, greater light and more facts will be brought to bear if more than one person is involved. Also, the leader will spot his creative thinkers and those who think conceptually. This will be of great value when he is looking for future leaders to train.

During this time the leader will do well to keep his thoughts to himself. If he says what he thinks, it might stifle discussion. He should just sit there intelligently ignorant, take it all in, gain what light he can, and let the people talk. Solomon said, "There is an appointed time for everything . . . a time to be silent and a time to speak." He reminds us, the wise heart "knows the proper time and procedure" (Ecc. 3:1, 7; 8:5).

5. *Narrow the field.* After a number of solutions have been offered, it is wise for you to arrange some sort of a "balance sheet." Try to think through all the possible consequences of the solutions offered. This will narrow the field somewhat.

In looking at all the possible solutions, the leader must guard against the advisor who thinks he knows it all and wonders why the leader doesn't take immediate action. This is often the guy who has pat answers, and who wonders, "Why make a Federal case out of this? We did it this way in the '60s—why not now?" He fails to realize what worked in the '60s might not be right for the '80s. The leader must take time to consider all the alternatives suggested by his advisors.

6. *Wait on God*. When this is done, it is time for you to take the next step—waiting on God. Pray, committing the whole matter to the Lord. "Commit your works to the Lord, and your plans will be established" (Prov. 16:3). The vital energizing union of faith and prayer will enable you to establish your thoughts in the will of God. The glory of God must be at the core. But waiting on God is not easy.

Yes, it is important that the leader sort out the real issue. And it is important that he receive counsel and look for the best solutions and alternate routes. But it is imperative that a leader wait on God. And here is the great failing. In my conversations with people in leadership positions around the world, this is the area where most have the greatest struggle.

The leader awakes in the morning to the jangle of the alarm clock or the music of a clock radio. The children are soon noisily getting ready to face the day—at school or play. He travels to work amid the noise of traffic—bus, train, automobile. At work he is surrounded by the sounds of phones, typewriters, intercoms, whatever. And so it goes throughout the day. To be still before God is difficult. There are always places to go, people to see, and things to be done. But in spite of all this, the leader must pull back into a private place and wait on God.

The Prophet Isaiah said it well: "Those who wait for the Lord will gain new strength; they will mount up with wings like eagles, they will run and not get tired, they will walk and not become weary" (Isa. 40:31). We certainly see this in the lives of the prophets, apostles, and in our Lord Jesus Himself.

Naturally, the work must go on and often the leader must be occupied with other things. But he *must* spend some time each day alone before God. King David put it forcefully: "Wait for the Lord; be strong, and let your heart take courage; yes, wait for the Lord" (Ps. 27:14). This attitude of faith and dependence is a great antidote to anxiety and a fretful spirit. The leader who spends much time with God moves ahead with the confidence that the

Lord will establish his thoughts and lead him to the right decision.

7. *Make the decision*. When it is time for you to decide, make the decision. Solomon notes, "The mind of man plans his way, but the Lord directs his steps" (Prov. 16:9).

God has given us minds and He expects us to use them. He has given us the power of choice. We must think, pray, gather information, and do all that we can to discover the real problem and assess the situation clearly. However, while we do this, we must remember in the final analysis, it is the Lord who directs. "Many are the plans in a man's heart, but the counsel of the Lord, it will stand" (Prov. 19:21). David wrote: "The counsel of the Lord stands forever, the plans of His heart from generation to generation" (Ps. 33:11). And the Lord said through the Prophet Isaiah, "Remember the former things long past, for I am God, and there is no other; I am God, and there is no one like Me, declaring the end from the beginning and from ancient times things which have not been done, saying, 'My purpose will be established, and I will accomplish all My good pleasure' " (Isa. 46:9-10).

It is truly a mystery how God accomplishes His eternally ordained purposes through people to whom He has given mind, will, and responsibility. Man is not a puppet. He has a free will to make his own decisions. Yet God is in charge and moves all things toward His purposes. Good decisions are a team effort that employ man's free will and God's sovereignty. We have to wisely plan our way; but in doing this, we need to rely on God's direction.

The leader will gain the confidence and respect of his people if they see this mark of prudence displayed in his life. If they see that he understands his job and is conscientious in his work, they will follow gladly. When wisdom is the hallmark of his speech and actions, they will join in to accomplish the task.

But they also need to see displayed a total trust in God. The leader should not be caught leaning on his own understanding.

8. *Follow through*. The last thing left is for you to implement the solution. Again this is a team effort.

Paul reminded us, "I can do all things through Him who strengthens me" (Phil. 4:13). "I can" expresses the human element of proceeding with discretion and wisdom. "Through Christ" expresses total dependence on God in faith.

Included in the immediate follow-through are these matters: What needs to be done immediately? Who is the best person to fill the job? When does it need to be accomplished? What will it cost?

High morale and enthusiasm in the ranks accompany the leader who is diligent to lead the people down the right paths, in constructive and productive service for their Lord. No one feels comfortable following a person who continually makes wrong decisions. An effective leader knows how to make good decisions.

10
Be a Competent Leader

Let's suppose you are a member of a football team. Suddenly, the coach becomes ill and resigns. You have some important games coming up, and you and the other players wonder what is going to happen to the team. Then one morning the sponsor of the team gets the players together and informs you that he has located a coach. Soon you meet the coach and begin your practice sessions.

The coach has many admirable qualities. He shows personal concern and interest in the players and their families. He is generous, gracious, and gregarious. He has a cheerful attitude, a pleasant smile, and really seems to enjoy being with the team. He works hard, is always on time, is available to the players, and gives himself unreservedly to the team. He laughs and jokes a lot, and keeps everyone in good spirits. Simply stated, he is an all-around good guy. But it soon becomes evident he has one glaring fault— he doesn't know anything about football. And that fact over-shadows all the rest. He can't do the job!

Some years ago I watched this happen in an organization. One of the men near the top was promoted and a new man was appointed to take his place. At first, everyone liked him. He had all the qualities of a good Boy Scout—he was trustworthy, loyal, helpful, friendly, courteous, kind, obedient, cheerful, thrifty, brave, clean, and reverent. Everyone settled in for a future of great productivity and success.

But it soon became evident that he was just not capable of leading his department. He didn't know the job. Most of the people in the department knew more than their boss. As a result people began to grumble. The department was going nowhere. All of their great plans began to fade in the dense fog of the man's inability to do the job. The people were totally demoralized and everything soon ground to a halt. The man had to be replaced.

That he exhibited many sterling qualities, was of upright moral character, and very likable, meant nothing anymore. Since he didn't know how to do his job, he was worthless to the enterprise.

A leader must lead. And to lead, he must know his job. Admittedly, he can fake it for a time but sooner or later it all catches up with him. When the people with whom he is involved begin to realize they are being led by a person who is unqualified and incompetent, they either leave, grumble and gripe, or force the man to leave. A leader's competence will help to make or break morale and motivation. The leader *must* know his job.

Solomon spoke to this. "The wisdom of the prudent is to understand his way, but the folly of fools is deceit" (Prov. 14:8). He was referring to the practical sense that can apply knowledge and experience to the job at hand. A prudent man understands what's involved, how to get from A to B, how to make the enterprise produce. And notice also that it is "his way" which he understands. The leader knows *his* job. He knows what it is that God wants *him* to do, and he sticks with that.

Temptations for the Leader

Not too long ago our Sunday School teacher referred us to Hebrews 12:1: "Therefore since we have so great a cloud of witnesses surrounding us, let us also lay aside every encumbrance, and the sin which so easily entangles us, and let us run with endurance the race that is set before us." As he expounded on this verse, I was struck with the words, *the race that is set before us*. Each of us has a race to run. Each of us has a job to do. Since it is obvious that we cannot do everything, it is then equally obvious that we must do what God gives us to do and leave the rest to someone else. That is not an easy thing to do. Our adversary often attacks us at this very point. And we as leaders are especially vulnerable. These attacks take several forms.

1. Envy. When the leader has contact with someone who does many things better than he does, he may envy the other person's talent. I fell into this trap on my first assignment with The Navigators. My wife and I were living in Pittsburgh, near the Rev. Ken Smith. Ken could sing like a lark. He had a vocabulary that was quite a contrast to my small town manner of speech. I tried to become like Ken, but it didn't work.

Many years later I was working alongside George Sanchez. George can also sing like a lark. He is a great song leader and master of ceremonies. When we would go on retreats, George could kick the football farther than I could. Fortunately, over the years I learned how to handle this sort of thing. I simply determined that I would stay with what God had given me to do and use the gifts God had given me. I learned to live and minister within my limits.

2. Pride. If the leader is gifted along a particular line, and does certain things well, he is tempted to hold in contempt those who are less gifted in that area. Some years ago the Lord gave me a verse that bore directly on this matter. The Apostle Paul admonished the Corinthians that they were not to be arrogant with one another. "For who regards you as superior? And what do you have that you did not receive? But if you did receive it, why do you boast as if you had not received it?" (1 Cor. 4:7) When a leader understands this principle, he is less likely to fall into the temptation of pride.

3. Guilt. As he is in fellowship with other Christian leaders, he observes them doing excellent works that are outside of his own calling from God. And this comparison can bring a sense of guilt.

Recently, my wife read an article on Mother Theresa of India. After reading it she came into the study and began to lament her own shallow dedication, compared with Mother Theresa's. The article had thrown her into a tailspin. After she talked for a while, we looked at 2 Corinthians 10:12: "For we dare not make ourselves of the number, or compare ourselves with some that commend themselves: but they measuring themselves by themselves, and comparing themselves among themselves, are not wise" (KJV). This passage speaks directly to the problem. When we compare ourselves among ourselves, we can go into defeat. We must simply measure ourselves against the path that God has chosen for us.

Everybody cannot be Mother Theresa. In fact, only one person can—Mother Theresa herself. Virginia cannot care for the starving people of India, but she can lead an evangelistic Bible study for the ladies in the neighborhood. This is one of the things God has given her, and her job is to do it well, under the power and wisdom of Christ.

Danger of Overstepping

The Scriptures are quite plain that it is dangerous to overstep the bounds of the call of God. Uzza reached out his hand to steady the ark of God and experienced the displeasure of the Lord (1 Chron. 13:9-10).

King Uzziah prospered mightily under the blessing of God "until he was strong. But when he became strong, his heart was so proud that he acted corruptly, and he was unfaithful to the Lord his God, for he entered the temple of the Lord to burn incense on the altar of incense" (2 Chron. 26:15-16). The Lord in His mercy tried to restrain Uzziah, but to no avail.

Then Azariah the priest entered after him and with him eighty priests of the Lord, valiant men. And they opposed Uzziah the king and said to him, "It is not for you, Uzziah, to burn incense to the Lord, but for the priests, the sons of Aaron who are consecrated to burn incense. Get out of the sanctuary, for you have been unfaithful, and will have no honor from the Lord God." But Uzziah, with a censer in his hand for burning incense, was enraged; and while he was enraged with the priests, the leprosy broke out on his forehead before the priests in the house of the Lord, beside the altar of incense.

And Azariah the chief priest and all the priests looked at him, and behold, he was leprous on his forehead; and they hurried him out of there, and he himself also hastened to get out because the Lord had smitten him. And King Uzziah was a leper to the day of his death; and he lived in a separate house, being a leper, for he was cut off from the house of the Lord. And Jotham his son was over the king's house judging the people of the land (2 Chron. 26:17-21).

Saul is another classic example of a leader who overstepped the bounds of his responsibilities, to offer a burnt offering unto the Lord. When Samuel asked him about it, Saul gave an interesting answer. He implied that he really didn't want to, but in light of the circumstances, he said, "I forced myself" to do it (1 Sam. 13:12). Samuel's answer is straight to the point.

You have acted foolishly; you have not kept the command-ment of the Lord your God, which He commanded you, for now the Lord would have established your kingdom over Israel forever. But now your kingdom shall not endure. The Lord has sought out for Himself a man after His own heart, and the Lord has appointed him as ruler over His people, because you have not kept what the Lord commanded you (1 Sam. 13:13-14).

The Apostle Paul said, "But I do not consider my life of any account as dear to myself, in order that I may finish my course, and the ministry which I received from the Lord Jesus, to testify solemnly of the Gospel of the grace of God" (Acts 20:24).

The leader must not let anything—pride, envy, guilt, or any other temptation—lure him from the path of service to which God has appointed him. It is not his business to be a judge or critic of what God leads others to do. Nor is it prudent for him to try to busy himself in another man's ministry. There are plenty of snares to avoid on his own path. There are ample roadblocks to overcome on his own path. Let him press toward the mark that God has set for him.

An athlete knows not only where the goal is, but also where the out-of-bounds markers are located. The leader will do well to keep both in mind. Paul certainly did. He wrote: "We, however, will not boast beyond proper limits, but will confine our boasting to the field God has assigned to us, a field that reaches even to you" (2 Cor. 10:13, NIV).

A Leader Never Knows It All

The leader who knows his job knows something else as well. He knows he never will get to the point where he can say he has arrived or knows it all. A good leader will continue to learn. "Wise men store up knowledge, but with the mouth of the foolish, ruin is at hand" (Prov. 10:14). Note the contrast Solomon made. One kind of person continually opened his mind and laid up knowledge. The other continually opened his mouth and laid out what was on his mind.

One of the marks of a good leader is that he is teachable and eager to learn those things that will improve his performance of the task he has received from the Lord. "The mind of the intelligent seeks knowledge, but the mouth of fools feeds on folly" (Prov. 15:14). An effective leader is never self-satisfied, but seeks every means to become more proficient, more knowledgeable, and better able to do the job.

Solomon had the wisdom to know that being a competent leader takes more than wisdom alone. The leader also needs faith. Wisdom deals with his understanding and skill. Faith goes far beyond that. It deals with what he can expect from God. To be sure, wisdom is necessary to the leader. Joseph's wise leadership and management saved an entire nation from starvation (Gen. 41:34-36). The apostles, through wise leadership and management, made provision for the needy and saved themselves from being sidetracked from their primary duties (Acts 6:1-4).

However, human understanding is not sufficient. The secret here is balance. The lazy leader might try to justify his sloth by saying, "I'm just leaving the whole matter to God." The frenetic leader can work and strive to the point he practically forgets he has a God. Through his own wisdom, he may bring a project to a successful outcome. But it is only as wisdom is mixed with a sincere faith in God that he finds happiness and satisfaction. (See Prov. 3:5-6; 16:20.)

Since it is obvious to an effective leader that he never "arrives" in his job performance, he will continually seek ways to improve. In addition, he must develop a lifestyle of trusting God. The most important means of achieving both of these objectives is an ongoing study and application of the Word of God. "From Thy precepts I get understanding; therefore I hate every false way" (Ps. 119:104). God's Word is the source for knowing the right thing to do and then doing it.

Seminars and books that deal with management and financial matters are helpful in building a leader's job knowledge. If the leader will be alert to available resources, and if he is selective, he will profit much from them. However, nothing beats the Word of God as a source of wisdom. "Thy commandments make me wiser than my enemies, for they are ever mine. I have more insight than all my teachers, for Thy testimonies are my meditation. I understand more than the aged, because I have observed Thy precepts" (Ps. 119:98-100).

Solomon called attention to another means of gaining guidance and understanding: "The way of a fool is right in his own eyes, but a wise man is he who listens to counsel" (Prov. 12:15). The leader should make it a practice to listen to those to whom he reports, to his peers, and to those people for whom he is responsible. Time and time again, godly counsel has been used to save leaders from the serious consequences of an unwise act. Moses was certainly much better off after he heeded the counsel of Jethro (Ex. 18:14-24). Also, David was saved from his folly by the restraining counsel of Abigail (1 Sam. 25:23-32).

Recently, I had lunch with a missionary who is being mightily used of God among university students in Mexico. It all began at an Inter-Varsity Christian Fellowship Urbana Missionary Convention in the 1960s. While a student at the University of Texas, he had gone to the convention, hopeful that God would open the way for him to serve in a foreign land. He had been a Christian for something over three years, and was moderately successful in witnessing for Christ on the campus. However, he was discouraged by the lack of follow-through by those whom he had won to Christ. During the convention he met Bill, a student from Texas A & M. Bill was about his same age—and was also interested in serving the Lord as a Christian worker when he graduated. But there was one difference. This Aggie had six other students with him from A & M. He had won two of them to Christ; those had won two more, and those in turn had won two others. It was a graphic demonstration of the very thing that Dan was looking for.

Dan spent the next morning with Bill, asking him questions about his ministry at Texas A & M. He asked how he could get the kind of help in his Christian life and service that would prepare him to do the same sort of thing at the University of Texas. Bill told him that if he would drive from Bryan, Texas to Austin once a week, he would pass along to him what he had been taught. It would be a sacrifice for the both of them, and difficult to work into an already crammed schedule. But this was exactly what Dan had longed for. So once a week for the next year, Dan drove those 80 miles to learn basic principles of witnessing and disciple-making. He listened to Bill, and applied what he learned.

Today Dan is a successful missionary, surrounded by a stalwart band of Latin American laymen who are highly effective in reaching their peers for Christ and training them in a life of discipleship. Dan knows his job and those who work with him are a highly motivated band of men and women whose morale remains high. It is a living example of Solomon's words, "Poverty and shame shall be to him that refuseth instruction: but he that regardeth reproof shall be honored" (Prov. 13:18, KJV).

A Leader Knows His Job

Nothing is more important for a leader than knowing his job. A few summers ago, while traveling in Europe, I had lunch in a restaurant in Oldenburg, Germany. There was a notice in the window saying that they honored the American Express Card. However, when I tried to use mine to pay the bill, no one in the restaurant knew how to run the machine to record the charge.

That same summer I was driving down a motorway in Holland. A friend who was traveling with me pointed out a large, modern office building that was empty. It had been erected too close to some large gasoline storage tanks. There was an ordinance that office buildings had to be so many meters from tanks such as those. Thousands of dollars were lost. The man who issued the permit did not know his job.

Recently, our family attended a concert held in our church. The pianist had a girl sitting beside her on the piano bench to turn the pages of music. As I watched her turn the pages, I asked myself a question: *How much does a person need to know to turn the pages of a book?* Very little, of course. In fact, my little granddaughter can do that. But she couldn't have done it for the pianist at the concert. The girl at the concert had to know how to read music. There was more to it than the ability to turn pages. She had to know *when* to turn them. And that took training.

A Leader Finishes a Job

Beginning a job can be exciting. Doing a job can be fun and fulfilling—but *only* if you know that there is every likelihood that you will be able to see it through to completion. To begin a job that you know is doomed to failure is demoralizing. It is the leader's responsibility to help the people accomplish the task. This presupposes he knows what he is doing and is capable of helping those who are involved with him to learn the task and bring it to a successful conclusion.

Jesus Christ is our prime example here. In His high priestly prayer He said, "I glorified Thee on the earth, having accomplished the work which Thou hast given Me to do" (John 17:4). He knew His task, He completed His task, and He trained His disciples to carry on the task after His departure.

Good intentions can't replace good performance. Every leader must be competent in the job God has given him to do. In approaching his task, he will do well to follow Solomon's example:

In Gibeon the Lord appeared to Solomon in a dream by night;

and God said, "Ask what you wish Me to give you."

Then Solomon said, "Thou hast shown great loving-kindness to Thy servant David my father, according as he walked before Thee in truth and righteousness and upright-ness of heart toward Thee; and Thou hast reserved for him this great loving-kindness, that Thou hast given him a son to sit on his throne, as it is this day. And now, O Lord my God, Thou hast made Thy servant king in place of my father David; yet I am but a little child: I do not know how to go out or come in. And Thy servant is in the midst of Thy people which Thou hast chosen, a great people who cannot be numbered or counted for multitude. So give Thy servant an understanding heart to judge Thy people to discern between good and evil. For who is able to judge this great people of Thine?"

And it was pleasing in the sight of the Lord that Solomon had asked this thing (1 Kings 3:5-10).

If you are responsible for an enterprise and you don't know what to do, ask God for wisdom, as Solomon did, and God will give it to you. For God wants competent leaders.

II
Be a Unifying Leader

I first became aware of the advantage of working together as a team while I was helping on my brother Everett's farm during my high school years in Iowa. We had two teams of horses—Molly and Bess, and Bud and Nance. Molly was a huge horse. Bess was much smaller and much older than Molly. When we hitched them to the cultivator and headed for the field, they functioned perfectly. Molly seemed to realize that Bess needed a little extra help at times and managed somehow to give it. She would put out a bit more on the turns and sort of carry Molly along. They were easy to manage because they worked so well together.

Bud and Nance were different. They were individuals to the core, and didn't pull well together. They seemed bent on making life miserable for each other. In spite of the fact that they were younger, stronger, and filled with a greater vitality than Molly and Bess, they did not do nearly as much work in a day. Their problem was that they had never learned to function well as a team.

As I spent those summers cultivating corn, it became clear to me why our high school basketball team never did very well. Individually, we were all pretty good players. We had a good, tall center, some quick forwards, and two fairly tough guards. But we never went anywhere. We would win some games, but we were usually eliminated during the first or second game at the county tournament. Our problem? We all tried to be a bunch of superstars. Being high-point man in the game seemed more important to us than winning the game. So we took spectacular shots, made fancy passes, and spent the games showing off our individual skills. The coach would try to settle us down, but we still played for personal recognition rather than team accomplishment. We loved to win, but we were our own worst enemies. We beat ourselves by our individual antics and refusal to be a functioning team. Also, I know now that our coach was letting us lead the team, instead of him being our leader.

After graduation from high school, I had the opportunity to join the marine corps, and considered this a golden opportunity. All during my high school years I had been the skinniest guy in school, and an easy mark for the school bullies. I couldn't defend myself, so I learned to outrun the guys who wanted to pick a fight. But all the while I dreamed of being big and muscular. I knew the marines were supposed to be a tough outfit and when I was accepted, I was elated. I just knew they would make a tough guy out of me. I even had a nickname picked out for myself—Nails. Nails Eims. It had sort of a ring to it. I could just see people looking at me as I swaggered down Main Street of Neola, Iowa, and whispering to each other, "Here comes Nails!" So I joined the marines, fully expecting them to transform me into an American Tarzan.

However, quite the opposite happened. I soon discovered that they were totally consumed with the idea of ending World War II. My grand and glorious plans for myself were not even in their thinking, because they were out to defeat the enemy. So I wound up as a machine gunner on an armored amphibious tank crew.

Each of us on the crew knew his job. Mine was operating the radio and the air-cooled 30-caliber machine gun. The driver knew his job as did the ammo man, the turret gunner, and the tank commander. No one played for himself. We were a team. Our lives depended on each other, and each of us had to do his job. By the way, I didn't become a muscular giant, and nobody ever called me Nails. My nickname in the marines was Chick. I was still the smallest one of the bunch, but as a member of that tank team, it didn't matter. I was just as important as the next guy. For we needed and trusted each other.

Solomon stated this principle succinctly and clearly: "Two are better than one because they have a good return for their labor. For if either of them falls, the one will lift up his companion. But woe to the one who falls when there is not another to lift him up" (Ecc. 4:9-10). If the leader can help those who co-labor with him to learn this truth, he is doing a service both to the group and to the kingdom of God. A bunch of individuals going off in their own directions, doing their own things, will accomplish little. But people banded together toward a common objective, supporting each other, caring for one another, praying for and loving each other, can be a mighty force for God. Individuals who stand alone are exposed to temptations that they would not be exposed to in the midst of a team. There is mutual warmth in the fellowship, and a greater strength for spiritual warfare, and for the work of Christ.

David said, "Behold, how good and how pleasant it is for brothers to dwell together in unity. . . . For there [where brethren are united] the Lord commanded the blessing—life forever" (Ps. 133:1-3).

This is something I have observed over the years. People who are united in heart and mind receive the blessing of God on their lives and ministry. This united spirit is certainly one of the keys that unlocks the blessing of God and unleashes the power of God. Without this, the group invariably falls into disarray; morale sinks, and whatever motivation they had disappears.

I'm certain that unity was one of the prime reasons for the prayer of the Apostle Paul: "Now may the God who gives perseverance and encouragement grant you to be of the same mind with one another according to Christ Jesus; that with one accord you may with one voice glorify the God and Father of our Lord Jesus Christ" (Rom. 15:5-6). Paul here revealed the grand purpose of unity: the glory of God. Obviously, the Lord is not glorified by group squabbles, disharmony, or contention. What glorifies God is like-mindedness and unity. Christian unity demonstrates that the group is controlled by the love and peace of Christ. Paul reminded the Philippians: "Only conduct yourselves in a manner worthy of the Gospel of Christ; so that whether I come and see you or remain absent, I may hear of you that you are standing firm in one spirit, with one mind striving together for the faith of the Gospel" (Phil. 1:27).

Solomon suggested many things that influence togetherness and oneness in the group. Let's consider four destroyers and three builders of unity.

Four Destroyers of Unity

1. Slander. Solomon said, "He who conceals hatred has lying lips, and he who spreads slander is a fool" (Prov. 10:18). One of the most effective ways to destroy another person's effectiveness for Christ is to say things that will keep people from placing their confidence in him. This can be done through ridicule or through presenting the person in an unfavorable light by stating a suspicion as fact.

Some friends of mine were planning to go to the mission field after they graduated from college. One evening this couple had a little disagreement while they were entertaining the pastor and his wife for dinner. Some months later the pastor mentioned the incident to a friend of his who happened to be on the missionary selection board. Three years later the couple applied to the board to serve overseas. As the board was discussing the possibility of the couple going overseas, the board member said, "I hear they don't get along very well together." Fortunately, the Lord had another person on the board who knew the couple and was able to state emphatically that this was not true. They got along just great. Because of the slander of a man who didn't know them well, this couple was almost prohibited from going to the mission field.

2. Anger. Solomon said, "An angry man stirs up strife, and a hot-tempered man abounds in transgression" (Prov. 29:22). "Do not associate with a man given to anger; or go with a hot-tempered man, lest you learn his ways, and find a snare for yourself" (Prov. 22:24-25).

Anger is a contagious emotion, and can prove to be devastating to a group.

3. Pride. Solomon said, "Only by pride cometh contention; but with the well advised is wisdom" (Prov. 13:10, KJV). Pride sparks contention over who will have the preeminence. The problem with pride is its tenaciousness. Pride is a rugged enemy, and difficult to get rid of. For us to function together in a way that glorifies God and advances His kingdom, we must deal with this enemy. Solomon said, "Pride goes before destruction, and a haughty spirit before stumbling. It is better to be of a humble spirit with the lowly, than to divide the spoil with the proud" (Prov. 16:18-19).

Shortly after I became a Christian, I met a young singer who had a great voice—and knew it. His many fans predicted he would go far. He did—straight to the bottom. After a few years of basking in the praise and adulation of the crowds, and failing to maintain a practice routine, his voice began to lose its luster. He kept trying, but without success. I have no idea where he is today.

4. Envy. Solomon said, "Wrath is cruel, and anger is outrageous; but who is able to stand before envy?" (Prov. 27:4, KJV) Envy is a strange thing. It is stirred up by all the right things—a holy life, a successful ministry, a good family, well-behaved kids. All of these can fan the flames of envy in the heart.

Just before the death of Christ, Pilate said to the people, "Whom do you want me to release for you? Barabbas, or Jesus who is called Christ?" (Matt. 27:17-18) Christ's perfect life prompted envy so fierce that it led to His death. In a group, a spirit of envy can lead to all manner of problems. The leader must be on the alert for these destroyers and combat them before they destroy him, the people who work with him, and their mission.

Three Builders of Unity

1. Love. Solomon said, "Hatred stirs up strife, but love covers all transgressions" (Prov. 10:12). Hatred is like rust in the fender of a car. The rust can be eating away underneath and no one realizes it until too late. Recently, one of the pastors of our church had a fire in his home. He put it out, and went to sleep. But a spark was still smoldering between the walls. During the night, it began to burn and did a great deal of damage. That's how hatred works.

In contrast, love is right up front, right out in the open. Love leads a person to cover for his friends, not to expose them. Love finds a way to overlook things rather than to take offense. Love is eager to forgive and forget. Love is inventive, creative, and imaginative, and figures out ways to make the best of things. Love is the ultimate power. It never fails.

A man was complaining to a missionary about the mission's work in Africa. "How can you go to Africa and preach to them about love when there is so much injustice in your own country?" he demanded.

The mission leader's answer was classic. "We don't go in and preach to them about love. We go in and love them."

2. *Control.* Solomon said, "He who goes about as a talebearer reveals secrets, but he who is trustworthy conceals a matter" (Prov. 11:13). One of the laws of God was, "You shall not go about as a slanderer among your people" (Lev. 19:16). If you know something about another person in your group, that would in any way hurt him if it were generally known, you should keep it to yourself.

When I was a new Christian, I was greatly challenged by the Jepson family in Seattle. This marvelous Christian family had a rule: to never say anything about another person unless they said something good, positive, and constructive.

Let your heart be a vault in which anything that could damage another is safely locked away, never to see the light of day. "A worthless man digs up evil, while his words are as a scorching fire. A perverse man spreads strife, and a slanderer separates intimate friends" (Prov. 16:27-28).

I'm sure James had this in mind when he wrote, "The tongue is a small part of the body, and yet it boasts of great things. Behold, how great a forest is set aflame by such a small fire! And the tongue is a fire, the very world of iniquity; the tongue is set among our members as that which defiles the entire body, and sets on fire the course of our life, and is set on fire by hell'' (James 3:5-6).

Not long ago, as I was driving to work, I saw a sanitation truck, on the back of which were these words: ''Satisfaction guaranteed or double your garbage back!'' I laughed—and then thought of Proverbs 17:9: ''He who covers a transgression seeks love, but he who repeats a matter separates intimate friends.''

A true friend keeps some things to himself. I don't want my garbage back. Neither do I want it spread all over the neighborhood. A disciplined tongue can go a long way to maintaining harmony in the team. We would all do well to pray David's prayer: ''Set a guard, O Lord, over my mouth; keep watch over the door of my lips'' (Ps. 141:3).

3. Kindness. Solomon said, ''A wholesome tongue is a tree of life; but perverseness therein is a breach in the spirit'' (Prov. 15:4, KJV). This proverb carries the thought of controlled speech a step further. Here the person's tongue is not just harmless, but filled with a wholesome, healing, positive influence. When the person speaks, his words are a balm of blessing. ''There is one who speaks rashly like the thrusts of a sword, but the tongue of the wise brings healing'' (Prov. 12:18). If the air is filled with discord, he brings peace to the troubled waters. Where verbal thorns abound in the garden of discontent, he creates a paradise of joy and peace. Some people who would recoil at the thought of using a dagger against their fellowmen repeatedly pierce others with their swords of unkindness, malice, and thoughtless jesting. Kindness is a mark of the learned person.

It is also the mark of the godly person. Writing prophetic words of the coming Messiah, Isaiah recorded, ''The Lord God has given Me the tongue of disciples, that I may know how to sustain the weary one with a word'' (Isa. 50:4). Kindness should be a law that governs our speech. ''She opens her mouth in wisdom, and the teaching of kindness is on her tongue'' (Prov. 31:26).

A Leader's Responsibilities
Solomon suggested four responsibilities for the leader, which contribute directly to maintaining the harmony and unity needed to

keep people on target and motivated to accomplish the task.

1. Integrity. Solomon said, "The lips of the righteous feed many, but fools die for lack of understanding" (Prov. 10:21). If the leader is diligent to nourish his people, to help them learn, to assist them in their work, and to teach them the Word, he will be laying the foundation of harmony and peace. The people will know they are becoming wealthy in the truest sense of the word. Paul spoke of being "poor, yet making many rich" (2 Cor. 6:10). The people will be nourished in the words of faith as their leader draws from the treasure of the Word that dwells richly in his heart (Col. 3:16). He and the people will experience the true leadership described by Malachi:

> True instruction was in his mouth, and unrighteousness was not found on his lips; he walked with Me in peace and uprightness, and he turned many back from iniquity. For the lips of a priest should preserve knowledge, and men should seek instruction from his mouth; for he is the messenger of the Lord of hosts (2:6-7).

2. Restraint. Solomon said, "A gentle answer turns away wrath, but a harsh word stirs up anger" (Prov. 15:1). A leader must keep his cool in the midst of tumult and dissension. If he responds in kind to heated words, he will do nothing but spread the flame of dissent and disunity. If he yields to the temptation to justify himself, put another person in his place, or insist on the last word, he has lost the battle for peace.

Restraint is a peacemaker. He who exercises it wins two battles—over himself and over others. A peacemaker applies Romans 12:19: "Never take your own revenge, beloved, but leave room for the wrath of God, for it is written, 'Vengeance is Mine, I will repay, says the Lord.' " The leader's tongue must be disciplined and dedicated to God. "The discretion of a man deferreth his anger; and it is his glory to pass over a transgression" (Prov. 19:11, KJV).

3. Good humor. Solomon said, "A joyful heart is good medicine, but a broken spirit dries up the bones" (Prov. 17:22). The thoughts expressed in Hebrews 1:9 have always been a source of wonder to me. "Thou hast loved righteousness and hated lawlessness; therefore God, Thy God, hath anointed Thee with the oil of gladness above Thy companions." Even though Jesus was a Man of sorrows and acquainted with grief, He also exhibited more gladness than anyone around Him.

Recently, I attended a rather large convention of Christian leaders. I recall seeking out one man who was full of the blessing of God. I knew he would be—it is his lifestyle. He rejoices even in tribulation. God has used his merry heart to inspire and motivate me. I also recall studiously avoiding another man who was there. He is known for his gloom and doom. In every contact I have had with him, he has exuded a cranky, complaining spirit. The contrast was vivid.

4. Friendship. Solomon said, "A friend loves at all times, and a brother is born for adversity. . . . There is a friend who sticks closer than a brother" (Prov. 17:17; 18:24). A good leader is friendly to those in the group. I have read management books and military manuals that warn against this: "Don't get too close to your people." Of course this is nonsense. Jesus said, "No longer do I call you slaves; for the slave does not know what his master is doing; but I have called you friends, for all things that I have heard from My Father I have made known to you" (John 15:15). How close is He to us? Closer than a brother! He indwells us!

The leader who holds himself aloof will stimulate a chill in the group. The leader who reaches out in friendship will generate warmth. It is certainly worth the effort for the leader to love the unlovely, befriend the unfriendly, cheer those who are down, and compliment those who are giving their all. In so doing, he will build a team whose morale and motivation will be used of the Spirit of God to enlarge the kingdom of God.

Mutual Need

The value of a united team cannot be overstated. Together, all of us are better than some of us. All of us will do more and do it better than a few isolated individuals. I have a friend who teaches in a unique graduate school. The purpose of the school is to demonstrate to the pupils the value of a team effort. A myriad of problems is presented for the class to solve. In one case, each class member is given the problem to work on individually. After a specified time, each person is placed on a team to talk the problem over—share ideas and then work on the problem together. Without exception, when the team tackles the problem together, they arrive at better solutions than any of the individuals did when they worked on it separately.

God has placed us in a body—the body of Christ. It is His purpose to demonstrate to us our interdependence on each other.

But now there are many members, but one body. And the eye cannot say to the hand, "I have no need of you"; or again the head to the feet, "I have no need of you.". . . That there should be no division in the body, but that the members should have the same care one for another. And if one member suffers, all the members suffer with it; if one member is honored, all the members rejoice with it. Now you are Christ's body, and individually members of it (1 Cor. 12:20-21, 25-27).

12
Be a Working Leader

Solomon was a multitalented individual. He was a builder, a leader, a manager, a decision-maker, a goal-setter, and much more. He was wise. He modeled the attributes of one who could maintain morale and motivate the masses. He built a huge fortune and ruled a mighty kingdom.

But above all else, he was a teacher.

In addition to being a wise man, the Preacher also taught the people knowledge; and he pondered, searched out, and arranged many proverbs. The Preacher sought to find delightful words and to write words of truth correctly. The words of wise men are like goads, and masters of these collections are like well-driven nails; they are given by one Shepherd'' (Ecc. 12:9-11).

As we reflect on Solomon's life, however, we are struck with an awesome truth. All that he had has since vanished. His mighty fleet, his great herds, his glorious temple, his great wealth, his beautiful home, and his kingdom are gone. But that which he taught remains.

If a leader is wise, he will glean a great lesson from this. There is much the leader can do—most of which will decay and vanish with the coming of tomorrow. But that which he teaches and builds into the lives of people will last, especially if his vision is strong enough to project itself beyond the immediate. And, if he understands the necessity of teaching those he instructs to be teachers of others, others who in turn will continue to repeat the process.

This was the genius of the Apostle Paul. He summarized his vision: "The things which you have heard from me in the presence of many witnesses, these entrust to faithful men, who will be able to teach others also" (2 Tim. 2:2). In this passage, Paul set forth his aim. He was committed to equipping laborers who could carry on the ministry that God had entrusted to him—the ministry of evangelizing the lost, establishing the saved, equipping spiritually qualified laborers for the harvest, and training competent leaders to carry on the ministry when he eventually would pass from the scene.

In the chapters of this book, we have discussed many things that a Christian leader should do. But what is the objective of all these things? These attributes and objectives of an effective leader are not ends in themselves. They are tools for accomplishing the task. This chapter presents the goal of Christian leadership—multiplying laborers for the vast and overripe harvest.

Unless people are won to Christ, there is no one to establish in the faith. But if a leader aims his personal ministry primarily at evangelizing the lost, he will accomplish only what one person can do. If he aims his ministry at multiplying laborers, he will see what a host of competent, trained, motivated men and women can accomplish.

The Leader as Laborer

Does that mean the leader should not evangelize the lost or establish the saved? Of course not. He himself is a laborer in the harvest, and must never forget that. If he quits laboring in the harvest, he will lose his prime teaching tool—setting an example for others to follow. Let us be very clear on this point—the leader is a laborer all the days of his life.

When the Bible refers to a laborer, what is it describing? For a partial answer to that question, we can look at a statement of Jesus.

"But when He saw the multitudes, He was moved with compassion on them, because they fainted, and were scattered abroad, as sheep having no shepherd. Then saith He unto His disciples, 'The harvest truly is plenteous, but the laborers are few; pray ye therefore the Lord of the harvest, that He will send forth laborers into His harvest' " (Matt. 9:36-38, KJV).

A laborer is one who is directly related to the harvest. We recognize there are laborers of *many* kinds in the work of the church, but for our purposes we will concentrate our attention on this *one* kind—the harvest worker.

The word that Jesus used is the word *ergatēs*, which means "a farmer, one who works in the fields." This truth is hard for some Christian leaders to accept. They visualize themselves at the other end of the spectrum. Rather than being out in the hot, dusty field doing the work of field hands, they see themselves behind huge desks in air-conditioned offices, jotting off memos to others who labor. But the Bible makes no provision for this kind of leader. The Seventy were laborers. The Apostles were laborers. Jesus Himself was a laborer. "We must work the works of Him who sent Me, as long as it is day; night is coming, when no man can work" (John 9:4). Paul told Timothy, "Be diligent to present yourself approved to God as a workman who does not need to be ashamed, handling accurately the Word of truth" (2 Tim. 2:15).

Jesus led His team into a vast, overripe harvest. "It came about that when Jesus had finished giving instructions to His disciples, He departed from there to teach and preach in their cities" (Matt. 11:1).

Paul did the same. "And according to Paul's custom, he went to them, and for three Sabbaths reasoned with them from the Scriptures" (Acts 17:2).

A leader who would follow the example of Christ and of the disciples whom He selected and trained, must labor and train others to do the same. Paul says we are laborers together with God (1 Cor. 3:9). He wrote to the Thessalonicans about their work of faith and their labor of love (1 Thes. 1:3). He called Epaphroditus his brother and fellow-worker (Phil. 2:25). He admonished the

church to "appreciate those who diligently labor among you, and
have charge over you in the Lord" (1 Thes. 5:12). He called elders
"those who work hard at preaching and teaching" (1 Tim. 5:17).
He reminded the Colossians of Epaphras who was "always laboring earnestly for you in his prayers" (Col. 4:12). We are called to
be laborers.

We gather from all this that witnessing is work, discipling is
work, training laborers is work, leadership is work, preaching is
work, and praying is work. All of these are directly related to the
plentiful harvest.

The Leader as Equipper

The leader is a laborer, first, last, and always. But more than that,
he is a laborer *plus*. For he is a laborer who also trains others to
labor. Not only is he skilled in winning the lost and building up the
saved, but he also knows how to equip others to do the same. So
we might call him an *equipper*.

An equipper is one who can help disciples become laborers. The
Apostle Paul wrote, that God "gave some as apostles, and some as
prophets, and some as evangelists, and some as pastors and
teachers, for the *equipping* of the saints for the work of service, to
the building up of the body of Christ" (Eph. 4:11-12).

A study of the Greek word *katartizō*, here translated "equip,"
opens up a treasure chest of practical help for the leader who is
serious about becoming a wise master builder, a skilled equipper, a
faithful man who is able to teach others. Its shades of meaning are
many. Greek scholars tell us that *katartizō* means "to complete
thoroughly, repair, adjust, fit, frame, mend, make perfect, perfectly join together, prepare, restore, and furnish completely."

Paul reminded the Ephesians that God had provided them with
certain divinely appointed leadership whose job it was to get them
ready to do quality work in the kingdom of God.

It is the leader's task to ensure that the workers are skillful in
their use of the Bible, highly motivated, and committed to the task
of laboring long and hard in the vast, overripe harvest that sur-
rounds them.

The same word is used in 1 Peter 5:10: "And after you have suffered for a little, the God of all grace, who called you to His eternal glory in Christ, will Himself perfect, confirm, strengthen, and establish you." Translated here as "perfect," it means "to fit you out completely," "to make you whole," "to make you what you ought to be."

Don Enright is a friend of mine who lives in Colorado Springs. He is an outstanding artist who specializes in drawing wild animals. For years he has concentrated his talent on the bighorn sheep that inhabit the Rocky Mountains. A few years ago, he decided to broaden his range and include the wild beasts of Africa. To prepare for the task, he took his camera and joined an African safari. At base camp they equipped or outfitted their party for their trek into the bush. They needed medicines, first aid equipment, food, tents, rifles, ammunition, and men to carry the supplies. That's how Peter used the word *katartizō*. As one would outfit a safari, the God of all grace—the Author and Finisher of our faith—works to outfit our lives for His glory.

The word is used again in Mark 1:19 and is translated "mending." Here the word means "to repair, overhaul, to make ready for use." James and John were repairing their nets and getting them in order.

In this sense, the leader is likened to a repairman. When we need car repair, in some cases we just need a minor adjustment—replacing a fuse or tightening a bolt. But sometimes it means a major overhaul. The mechanic must be able to do both in order to enable the automobile to function at its best. And so the leader must have the compassion and skill to take the broken or bruised lives and make whatever major or minor repairs are needed to get them functioning again in perfect order.

Paul expressed a similar idea to the Thessalonians: "We night and day keep praying most earnestly that we may see your face, and may complete what is lacking in your faith" (1 Thes. 3:10). The word *complete* means "mending the gaps in faith, filling in that which is lacking."

When my youngest son was in junior high school, he was given a large poster and a box of colored pencils. He was supposed to follow the instructions and paint the picture. There were scores of colors involved and it was quite a complicated task. So he began. Night after night he worked on his project. He would do the reds, then the blues, then the greens, and so on. One by one he filled in the gaps and finally the picture was complete. It took weeks to complete, but he finally made it, and it was beautiful. That's the thrust of the word here. Possibly, there are certain misunderstood doctrines that the leader must teach simply and clearly. He may strengthen people's faith in the promises of God or help them learn how to study the Bible for themselves. Wherever there are gaps, the leader must take whatever action is necessary to see that they are filled in.

In Hebrews 11:3, we see another meaning of *katartizō:* "By faith we understand that the worlds were prepared by the Word of God, so that what is seen was not made out of things which are visible." *Prepared* means "to arrange, to place in proper order." In the beginning, the world was without form and void. There was confusion and emptiness. But out of this shapeless, useless mass, this rough draft, God brought forth a world of perfect order that functions perfectly according to His divine plan and law. This should be of great encouragement to the leader. If God can do it with His world, He can do it with His people. I have talked with leaders who looked on their people and saw confused, useless, empty lives. By God's power, His wisdom, His Word, and His Spirit, mighty and dramatic changes can be wrought. Confusion can be turned to purpose. Uselessness can be changed to productivity.

Luke gives us another facet of the word. "A pupil is not above his teacher; but everyone, after he has been fully trained, will be like his teacher" (Luke 6:40). Here is the idea of growth. The leader is to help the people grow in grace and the likeness of Christ. He must teach them to pray and to read and memorize the Word, in order to establish a daily and meaningful fellowship with the Saviour. All too often the leader relies only on his teaching to accomplish the task. And all too often, that doesn't work.

Yes, people need to be taught. But Jude added the missing ingredient. "But you, beloved, building yourselves up on your most holy faith; praying in the Holy Spirit; keep yourselves in the love of God, waiting anxiously for the mercy of our Lord Jesus Christ to eternal life" (Jude 20-21).

They must be taught means to mature and to keep themselves in the love of God. If the leader can help his people learn how to dig into the Word for themselves, to write it on the tables of their hearts through Scripture memory, to establish the practice of morning prayer and Bible reading, he will do much to help them grow and develop into all that God wants them to be.

In Galatians 6:1, we see another use of *katartizō*. "Brethren, even if a man is caught in any trespass, you who are spiritual, restore such a one in a spirit of gentleness; looking to yourselves, lest you too be tempted." Here the leader who is controlled by the Holy Spirit must redirect the wanderer and gently set him right. The word is used here in a medical sense, to reset, as in the case of a dislocated bone. A dislocated limb cannot function properly. A person out of joint in the body of Christ could be lost to effective service in the kingdom of God.

Some years ago the following notice appeared in our newspaper:

THREE YOUTHS HURT IN AUTO ACCIDENT

Three youths were injured when their car left U.S. 24 near Green Mountain Falls and plummeted 323 feet down an embankment, rolling over twice, according to the State Patrol. Randy S. Eims, 17, was admitted to Penrose Hospital with a broken foot. Eims is in satisfactory condition, a hospital spokesman said.

While Randy was sleeping in the back seat, the Volkswagen convertible in which he was a passenger suddenly left the road and rolled end over end down the embankment. I arrived at the hospital in time to see the doctor make arrangements to pop the bone back into place. He had the knowledge and the skill and the gentleness to do the job right. The next few weeks were quite an education for Virginia and me. Here was a muscular young man, a terror on the soccer field, a tiger on the tennis courts, and a picture of graceful coordination on the ski slopes, practically helpless. But eventually the foot healed and he was back in action.

That's the idea in this passage. The Apostle Paul was not speaking of a person in hot pursuit of sin, but of one who was injured. Now he was crippled and needed to be restored to health and service by someone who would manifest the fruit of the Spirit—love, gentleness, and meekness being prime requisites.

In Hebrews 13:20-21 we see *katartizō* relating to the will of God. "Now the God of peace, who brought up from the dead the great Shepherd of the sheep through the blood of the eternal covenant, even Jesus our Lord, equip you in every good thing to do His will, working in us that which is pleasing in His sight, through Jesus Christ, to whom be the glory forever and ever. Amen."

It is true that no one will grow to his fullest maturity, or come to his place of greatest service for Christ, if he is constantly in doubt as to the will of God for his life. But if he is confident that he knows what God wants him to do, he is highly motivated to receive the instruction and training he needs. A leader who is ready, willing, and able to help prepare others to do the will of God will render a great service to His kingdom. Some people need to discover God's will. Others need to prepare themselves to do it. With yet others, it is a combination of both. Once again we clearly see the need for discernment, patience, and skill in the life of the leader. He must spend much time on his knees before God, and with the open Bible, if he would be effective in this ministry of equipping others to discern and accomplish God's will for their lives.

Paul used the word again in his letter to the Corinthians: "Now I exhort you, brethren, by the name of our Lord Jesus Christ, that you all agree, and there be no divisions among you, but you be made complete in the same mind and in the same judgment" (1 Cor. 1:10). This speaks of the unity of believers. A bickering, jealous, suspicious body of believers is of little use to the Holy Spirit in advancing the cause of Christ. Jesus prayed, "That they may all be one; even as Thou, Father, art in Me, and I in Thee, that they also may be one in Us; that the world may believe that Thou didst send Me" (John 17:21). The prayer of Paul was that there would be no factions and divisions, but that they would be solidly joined together in mind and thought. To build unity is not easy. To keep it can be even harder. The devil is always on the lookout to drive some wedge between the brothers and sisters in Christ and render them useless to the purpose of God. To keep the unity of the Spirit in the bond of peace requires work, prayer, admonition, and encouragement.

The last verse we will consider is 2 Corinthians 13:9. "For we rejoice when we ourselves are weak but you are strong; this we also pray for, that you may be made complete." The thought here is the all-around strengthening and development of Christian character.

Perseverance

Katartizō has to do with "fitting out," "overhauling," "filling in the gaps," "placing in order," and in a medical sense, "setting a joint in place." All of this is done for the purpose of helping people do the work that God has given them, to help them grow strong in the Lord and the power of His might, to discern and do the will of God, to live in unity, and to develop godly Christian character.

There are two ways the leader can look at these tasks—in despair or in dependence. He can see the job, and throw up his hands in frustration. Or he can see his limitations, his lack of experience and knowledge, and ask, "Who is sufficient for these things?"

The Apostle Paul said: "Not that we are adequate in ourselves to consider anything as coming from ourselves, but our adequacy is from God, who also made us adequate as servants of a New Covenant, not of the letter, but of the Spirit; for the letter kills, but the Spirit gives life" (2 Cor. 3:5-6). He must persevere and remain at the task he has been given.

One of the finest examples I ever saw of perseverance was on the island of Fiji. My wife and I were in a bus on our way to the airport. We had gotten a late start and the driver was doing all he could to make up time and get the passengers to their flight. The rain was blowing in through the broken windows as we bounced along. At the foot of a hill, we came behind a slow-moving cement truck. Our driver was clearly agitated at this stroke of bad fortune and tried to pass. But to no avail. Oncoming traffic kept him behind the cement truck for miles and miles. Finally, with a break in the traffic, the driver passed the truck, and we bounced down the road at top speed. But then the driver spotted a small boy standing in the middle of the road, and carrying a tin sign. He was on school patrol, to stop the traffic and permit the children to cross the road. The little tin sign said, "Stop." But our bus driver was in no mood to stop.

The lad saw him coming at breakneck speed and started to run for the ditch. But the boy's sense of duty prevailed. He turned, faced the oncoming bus, and stood his ground. At the last minute, when he saw he could not win, the driver slammed on his brakes. The bus slid to a stop and the uniformed school children passed safely across the road. The lad had persevered and had won the test of wills. By the way, we arrived at the airport just in time to get on the plane.

Reward

Let me assure you of this: equipping people to be and do their best for Christ may be a tough, demanding, and sometimes thankless job, but it is worth it. The truth of this was driven home to me some years ago when I was speaking at a servicemen's conference on the island of Okinawa. The chaplain had secured an abandoned radar site for our meetings. No other religious group had ever been permitted to use the site. Chaplain Boggs had put in many hours over many months and logged over 1,000 phone calls to get the place for us. On Saturday morning he came out to the conference and told us why he had worked so hard for us.

Some years before, he had been stationed at Ft. Riley, Kansas. One day, two soldiers came into his office and asked if they could help him in his work. They wanted to do evangelism in the barracks and form some Bible study groups. Chaplain Boggs was delighted. In a matter of weeks there were 19 men involved, and soon he was preaching to two full services on Sunday morning, rather than to one that was half empty. The outfit then was ordered to Vietnam, and on the ship going over, the two men who had talked with the chaplain at Ft. Riley came to him and asked if they could have a Bible study. Chaplain Boggs checked with the captain and secured permission.

A year later when the chaplain returned to the States, a minister came into his office and laid three letters on his desk. The letters were from the minister's son. This is what they said.

"Dear Dad, some guys on board ship have invited me to a Bible study. Think I'll go—thought it would please you."

The second said, "Dear Dad, we're in Vietnam now and I'm leading a Navigator Bible study."

The third one said, "Dear Dad, tomorrow is a big operation— don't know if I'll make it back. If I don't, thank The Navigators and Chaplain Boggs." Then the father asked if Chaplain Boggs would preach the funeral service for his son.

After telling us this story, Chaplain Boggs exhorted us to give our lives to equipping others to become laborers for Christ. He had seen how the Lord had used the two men who had first come to him at Ft. Riley. God had used them to revive his chapel services, to inspire many people to study the Word on their own, and to restore the minister's son to fellowship with the Lord. At one time, somebody had made an investment in the lives of these two men that paid rich dividends. As I listened to Chaplain Boggs tell the story, I was struck with the fact that the two soldiers in Chaplain Boggs' story were not professional Christian workers, but just two ordinary guys doing what somebody had previously equipped them to do.

Let me urge you to do the same. If there is one thing this world needs, it is spiritually qualified laborers who are proficient in bringing people to Christ, and who know:

• how to help them grow in the faith through daily fellowship with Christ;

• how to teach people how to study the Bible;

• how to memorize Scripture and encourage others to do the same;

• how to pray and help others establish a vital prayer life; and so on down the list of the spiritual basics. But there is one catch. You as leader must be setting the example.

If you give yourself to people in this way, you will be a leader who maintains motivation and morale among your people at the highest level. You will be investing your life in equipping laborers for the harvest all over the world. "The harvest is plentiful but the laborers are few" (Luke 10:2). Like every Christian you have a decision to make. You can watch others work, or you can join the ranks of God's laborers.